Bristol Railway Stations

BRISTOL
RAILWAY STATIONS AND HALTS
1840–2005

MIKE OAKLEY

redcliffe

First published in 2006 by Redcliffe Press Ltd.,
81g Pembroke Road, Bristol BS8 3EA

www.redcliffepress.co.uk

© Mike Oakley 2006

ISBN   1 904537 54 5
ISBN 13 9781904537540

British Library Cataloguing-in-Publication Data
A catalogue record for this book is available from the British Library

Typesetting by GCS, Leighton Buzzard, Bedfordshire.
Printed by The Charlesworth Group, Wakefield

Contents

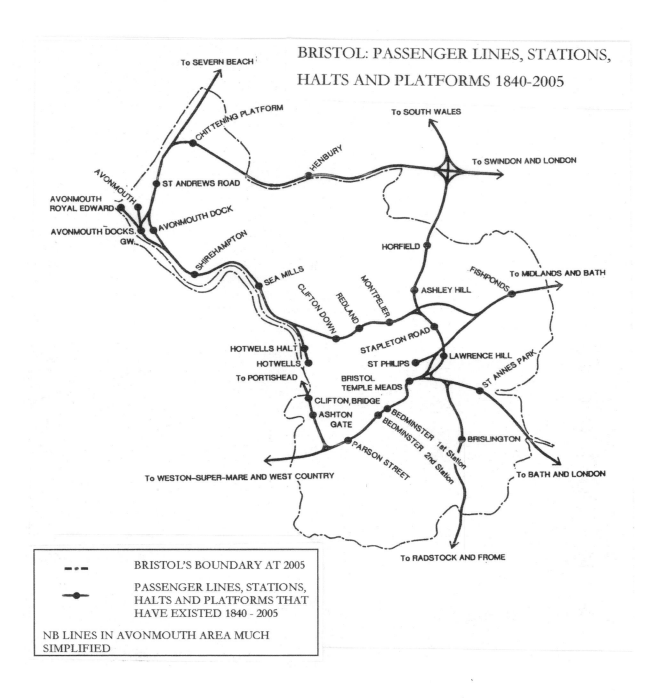

BRISTOL: PASSENGER LINES, STATIONS, HALTS AND PLATFORMS 1840-2005

Introduction

As we celebrate in 2006 the 200th anniversary of the birth of Isambard Kingdom Brunel (1806-1859), it is an opportune time to take a close look at Bristol's railway stations and halts. It is appropriate because one of Brunel's greatest legacies to the city is Temple Meads Station, the first section of which was designed and engineered by him for the Great Western Railway and completed in 1841. A number of extensions and alterations subsequently took place, in particular in the 1870s and 1930s, and today the station stands as one of Bristol's outstanding buildings, both architecturally and historically, a Grade I listed building.

The stations and halts of any city or town contribute a great deal to its physical, social and economic history and Bristol is a good example. In addition to Temple Meads, a further 25 stations and halts sited within today's city boundaries have served the residents and commercial life.

Many books have been published over the years on the railways of Bristol. Sixteen years ago the author, with Redcliffe Press, prepared and published *Bristol Suburban*, an account of the city stations and halts, issued to celebrate the 150th anniversary of the opening of Bristol Temple Meads. This new book builds upon and updates the 1990 book and includes many different photographs. A particular feature is the inclusion of a number of 'then and now' comparisons where a photograph has been taken at or very close to an earlier shot which in some cases dates back nearly 100 years. The contrast in the case of Temple Meads is relatively small but in many cases the change is very significant and perhaps sad. If many of these quite impressive buildings had survived until more recent years surely some good re-use could have been introduced.

The classic J Bourne 1846 drawing of Temple Meads. The view is looking west into the Train Shed section with the Engine and Carriage Shed beyond. Note the roof support columns close to the platform edge and the splendid roof. Manual shunting is in progress as a Fire Fly class locomotive is ready to depart towards Bath.

Bristol's Passenger Rail Network 1840-2005

The development of the railway network was an important part of British industrial and social history in the nineteenth and early twentieth centuries. The potential for this new form of transport was discussed in many places: Bristol businessmen, long dissatisfied with the bad road communications to London and also concerned at the many developments in the ports and other centres in the north of England, saw the railway as a solution to their problems. In the autumn of 1832 the Bristol Chamber of Commerce, the Merchant Venturers and other local industrial organisations formed a committee and prepared an ambitious proposal to build a railway to London. The committee acted quickly and money was advanced from many quarters. Isambard Kingdom Brunel, born 200 years ago in 1806, and designer of the Clifton Suspension Bridge, was appointed on the 7th March 1833 to design and supervise construction of a Bristol to London railway. A route was rapidly drawn up. A public meeting, held in Bristol on 30th July 1833 to consider Brunel's report, passed a resolution for the formation of a company, which very soon became the Great Western Railway Company (GWR). The Act for the construction of the line received Royal Assent on 31st August 1835 and work began almost immediately.

One of Brunel's chief ambitions was to build a line on which trains could travel at high speed and, with this aim in mind, he recommended a gauge of 7 ft 0¼ inch which became known as the broad gauge. This was a radical departure from the gauge already in use on other railways but the GWR directors accepted his recommendation, persuaded by arguments for the development of rolling stock and smoother running.

The first section of the GWR from London to Maidenhead opened on 4th June 1838 and by the end of 1840 there was a continuous line westward as far as Hay Lane close to Wootton Bassett in Wiltshire. During the late 1830s work was in hand on the Bristol to Bath section and much of the line was complete by August 1839. The following year saw the construction of the bridge over the Floating Harbour just east of the new terminus at Bristol Temple Meads. At just after 8 a.m. on 31st August 1840, five years to the day after the GWR Act received Royal Assent, the first train left Bristol for Bath drawn by the engine 'Fireball'. There was no other station then within the city and only one intermediate station at Keynsham. The first station within Bristol, at St Annes Park, did not open until 23rd May 1898, to serve the local housing development. The through line to London opened on 30th June 1841, following the completion of Box Tunnel which allowed running between Chippenham and Bath.

The promotion of a railway linking Bristol to London prompted action on a possible line to the west country. A month after the Act of Parliament had been passed authorising the GWR to build a line to London, Bristol merchants issued a prospectus for a railway to Exeter. The appropriate Act of Parliament was passed on 19th May 1836 incorporating the Bristol and Exeter Railway Company, whose aim was to run from a junction with the Great Western Railway at Temple Meads to meadows in the parish of St Thomas in Exeter. The decision was made again to build the line at broad gauge. Construction progress was faster in the northern section although it had originally been intended to open the whole line to Exeter at the same time. By the end of May 1841 the railway as far as Bridgwater was virtually complete and was opened on 14th June 1841, 16 days prior to the opening of the through Bristol to London route. The Bristol and Exeter Railway amalgamated with the GWR from 1st January 1876.

At the opening of the Bristol and Exeter Railway there were no intermediate stations within the city of Bristol. These eventually came to serve the developing Bristol suburbs: the first, at Bedminster, opened in 1871, an earlier excursion Platform had served passengers for some years. The second Bedminster station opened in 1884, some 250 yards to the west of, and replacing, the first station. Extensions to the second station took place in 1908 and complete rebuilding and enlargement came with the quadrupling of the line in 1932. Parson Street station was not opened until 29th August 1927 and, like Bedminster, it was rebuilt in association with the major track improvements in 1932-33.

The pattern of early radial routes out from

Bristol Temple Meads continued with the public opening of the broad gauge Bristol and Gloucester Railway on 8th July 1844. Once again the lack of initial suburban stations within the city was repeated and, indeed, the first and only example did not come until 1st April 1866 with the opening of Fishponds station. To relieve pressure on Temple Meads, a new station was later opened at St Philips on 2nd May 1870.

By the middle of the 1840s Bristol was thus linked by rail to London, the west country, the midlands and the north, but there was no direct route to South Wales. It was possible to travel by train between Bristol and Cardiff, but only via Gloucester, a distance of over 90 miles. A shorter route was urgently required.

An early attempt in the late 1840s proved unsuccessful. The project was revived by the Bristol and South Wales Union Company of 1857. An Act was passed for the construction of a new line between South Wales Junction on the main GWR line, half a mile east of Temple Meads, and New Passage Pier on the Severn Estuary, north of Severn Beach, from which a ferry ran to Portskewett Pier, where a branch linked to the South Wales line. Work began in October 1858 and a single track broad gauge line was opened ceremoniously on 25th August 1863 and to the public on 8th September 1863. For the first time in Bristol the new line, worked from its opening by the GWR, had from the outset two suburban stations, at Lawrence Hill and Stapleton Road. The line was converted to standard gauge in August 1873 and doubled throughout by 1885, in preparation for the opening of the Severn Tunnel. Further stations serving the Bristol suburbs opened at Ashley Hill on 13th August 1864 and Horfield on 14th May 1927. Both these were prompted by housing development in the north of Bristol.

Two further developments in the Bristol rail network were built parallel to the River Avon through the famous gorge. The year 1867 brought the opening of a branch line to Portishead, leaving the main west country line in the south west suburbs of Bristol and running north and north west along the western bank of the River Avon through the gorge. Built as a single track broad gauge line, this railway began operating to Portishead on 18th April 1867. The branch was built by the Bristol and Portishead Pier and Railway Company but worked by the Bristol and Exeter Company. One of the original stations on the Portishead branch was at Clifton Bridge, sited some half mile south of the landmark after which it is named. Ashton

Gate opened initially in 1906 to serve the crowds at Bristol City's nearby football stadium. This closed in 1917 but reopened in 1926.

Some two years before the opening of the Portishead branch had come the unusual isolated development of the Hotwells to Avonmouth line. During the nineteenth century Bristol's importance as a port declined, with the larger ships then coming into use being unable to navigate the bends on the river to the City Docks. In anticipation of possible new docks at the river mouth, the Bristol Port Railway and Pier Company (BPRP) was formed. This aimed to construct a new railway from Hotwells, under the then unfinished Suspension Bridge, to the mouth of the Avon where a new deep water pier was to be built. It was also hoped to develop leisure facilities to attract day visitors to the banks of the Severn. As it was not proposed to cater for anything but local traffic, no connections were thought necessary with any other railway at that time, a decision that the Company was later to much regret. The line opened on 6th March 1865 and at its opening there were stations, all within the city, at the Hotwells terminus itself (known as Clifton until March 1891), Sea Mills, Shirehampton and at Avonmouth. The BPRP was taken over by the GWR and Midland Railway (MR) on 1st September 1890. Later, on 14th May 1917, Hotwells Halt was opened, just north of the Hotwells terminus, being a wartime expedient for long trains that could not be accommodated at the terminus.

Soon after its opening it was realised that this local traffic was insufficient for the viability of the line and that if a major dock was to develop a rail link with the main lines, by that time radiating from Bristol, was essential. A direct route from Hotwells to the rail focus at Temple Meads was, by the 1860s, blocked by development and thus a new line, the Clifton Extension Railway, was proposed running from a junction with the Bristol Port Railway in the gorge below Sneyd Park, under Clifton Down and eastwards to the Ashley Hill area. At this point the line was to divide with a short link to the South Wales line north of Stapleton Road (Narroways Hill Junction) and a longer link to the Midland Railway line, approximately one mile to the east (Kingswood Junction). The new line was opened from the east for goods traffic only as far as Whiteladies Road in June 1874 and, on 1st October in the same year, passenger traffic commenced to this point with stations opening at Clifton Down itself and Montpelier. The station at Redland was not opened until 12th April 1897.

Work continued on the tunnel under Clifton Down and this was eventually opened to goods traffic on 24th February 1877, the same day as the new dock opened at Avonmouth. However, the line was not opened for passenger use through the tunnel for a further eight years, there being problems of signalling inadequacies and also of platform length at Sea Mills. Eventually on 1st September 1885 the Clifton Extension Railway was opened to passengers from Clifton Down to Avonmouth; on the same day the new Avonmouth Dock joint station was opened although services continued to the old Avonmouth terminus station of the Bristol Port Railway. Earlier facilities at Avonmouth Dock were provided before the opening of the dock itself.

The evolution of the rail network around Bristol had thus largely been completed by the mid-1870s but one blank area remained to be filled, that to the south and south east of the city. This was perhaps surprising in view of the coalfield development in the Radstock area. Following a number of financial and construction difficulties, the standard gauge Bristol and North Somerset Railway was opened to passengers and goods from Bristol to Radstock on 3rd September 1873. There was then one station within the current city boundary at Brislington, though at that time it was in Somerset.

The early years of the twentieth century saw the final important initiatives in the development of Bristol's railway network; these were to the north and north west of the city. First, along the banks of the Severn Estuary, plans had been considered for some years for a line to link the Avonmouth area with the South Wales line only 7 miles to the north. After a number of abortive attempts by smaller companies, the GWR decided to construct this important link itself and the line opened for freight traffic only on 5th February 1900. The extension of the Avonmouth Docks provided a major impetus to rail traffic in this part of the city, in particular with the opening of the new Royal Edward Dock in 1908. Two years later, on 29th April 1910, the new Royal Edward Dock passenger station opened at Avonmouth.

From 1877 (freight) and 1885 (passengers) the principal rail link to Avonmouth Docks from the main network was via the Clifton Down line; however, from 1900 freight traffic was also able to use the new link to the South Wales line northwards along the banks of the Severn Estuary. The opening, in 1903, of the GWR South Wales cut-off route from Wootton Bassett to Patchway provided an opportunity for a new cut-off to Avonmouth. A line was constructed from Stoke Gifford on the South Wales line westwards to the Avonmouth – Pilning line at Chittening, across the north of Bristol. This line, opening on 9th May 1910, was destined to play an important role in the development of traffic to and from the Avonmouth Docks.

In addition to being used for Docks traffic, the new line provided opportunities for new passenger facilities, serving settlements and suburbs along the northern edge of the city including a station at Henbury. The local trains on the new route initially terminated at yet another station at Avonmouth, a wooden platform near the dock gate known as Avonmouth Docks (GW). A platform was opened on the line at Chittening during the period 1918-1923 and again after the Second World War from 31st May 1948. A station opened at St Andrews Road on 1st March 1917; this was closed between November 1922 and June 1924 but remains open today on the Avonmouth to Severn Beach line.

The 1920s and 1930s saw a number of developments of the Bristol passenger rail network, both positive and negative. An example of the latter was the closure of the Hotwells Spur which, following the opening of the Clifton Down to Avonmouth line, had been a little-used branch southwards into the gorge. Traffic was never great and in the 1920s the Bristol Corporation, keen to improve road communications to the docks at Avonmouth, constructed the new Portway road which opened on 2nd July 1926. Some of the railway land was required and the spur line through the gorge closed in two sections – Hotwells to Hotwells Halt on 19th September 1921, and the remaining section as far as Sneyd Park Junction on the Clifton Down line on 3rd July 1922. This was an early example of a rail trackbed being subsequently used for a new road!

In contrast, however, on many of the lines in the Bristol area, traffic was at its busiest during the 1930s with railways still being much in demand and indeed fashionable for both passenger and freight traffic. Two principal developments took place in this period. First, there was the major reconstruction work at Bristol Temple Meads and secondly, at a number of locations, lines were re-laid and in some places widened. The tracks on the South Wales route north from Narroways Hill Junction to Filton were quadrupled, necessitating reconstruction of Ashley Hill and Horfield stations, both of these being reopened on 30th April 1933. Quadrupling of the track also took place to the south west of Temple

Meads station and required the reconstruction of Bedminster and Parson Street stations, these reopening in 1932 and 1933 respectively. During the Second World War the railways played a major role transporting troops, armaments and civilian traffic, the last including evacuees from cities including Bristol.

The post-1950 period saw withdrawal of passenger services from a number of lines in the Bristol area. The Bristol to Radstock line, including the station at Brislington, closed to passengers on 2nd November 1959 and this was followed by the Bristol to Portishead line which closed to passengers on 7th September 1964, including both Clifton Bridge and Ashton Gate, though the latter subsequently had temporary use by football supporters and also by travellers to a Mission held at Ashton Gate Stadium. Later in 1964 the Chittening to Stoke Gifford line closed to passenger services including Chittening Platform and Henbury station, on 23rd November. The final, most significant, closure in 1970 was that of the former Midland Railway Bristol to Mangotsfield and Gloucester line, running north east from Temple Meads station through the suburbs. The closure of the station at Fishponds to passengers had come in 1966, four years earlier.

There are three examples of suburban stations in Bristol that have closed on main lines which radiate from Temple Meads and which remain open for regular passenger trains. These are at Ashley Hill and Horfield on the main line to South Wales and the north, both closing on 23rd November 1964 and at St Annes Park on the main Bristol to Bath and London route which closed on 5th January 1970.

Local passenger services continue to run on the Bristol Temple Meads to Severn Beach line, serving suburban stations at Lawrence Hill, Stapleton Road, Montpelier, Redland, Clifton Down, Sea Mills, Shirehampton, Avonmouth Dock and St Andrews Road. In May 1989 Lawrence Hill and Stapleton Road resumed use as suburban stops on the Bristol to Gloucester services. The two other remaining suburban stations are at Bedminster and Parson Street on the line to Weston-super-Mare and the west country. The services at Bedminster are at a reasonable level but Parson Street has only a basic service in the morning and evening peak period, though slightly improved in recent years.

The Role of Bristol's Stations

The focus of Bristol's passenger rail network has always been, without dispute, Bristol Temple Meads in its roles of terminus, interchange point and departure point for scheduled trains and excursion traffic. It is only since the opening in 1972 of Bristol Parkway station, north of the city, that this role has been challenged, this coming particularly because of the availability of a large number of parking places and the quicker journey times to London via the Badminton cut-off route.

A number of other Bristol stations have nevertheless played a major role in passenger services, in particular as interchange points. The outstanding example of this was Stapleton Road which, for some years, not only served as the main Bristol station for South Wales to south coast trains not calling at Temple Meads, but was also an exchange point for passengers on the Clifton Down to Avonmouth line changing to trains both on the London route via Badminton and the South Wales to the south coast line. To a degree also, Fishponds had an interchange role with passengers transferring from trains on the Clifton Extension Railway to the Midland Railway en route to either the Midlands or Bath. This role, however, was less than that played by Mangotsfield, beyond the city boundary. Bedminster and Parson Street stations also had a minor exchange role for excursionists from the west country changing to trains along the gorge to Portishead.

Bristol's suburban stations also played a number of other roles: firstly as departure and arrival points for travellers to and from Temple Meads where they either transferred to long distance trains or walked to and from work in the city centre. In the latter role St Philips station also played a part. Secondly, suburban stations were also used extensively for movements to and from adjacent factories and other work places, for instance commuters working at Brislington, Fishponds and Avonmouth. Many workers also travelled from suburban stations in Bristol to the Fry's factory at Keynsham, after it was relocated from the city centre and also to the aircraft works at Filton and Patchway, north of the city.

Thirdly, excursion traffic was also important in passenger rail movements. Undoubtedly the busiest station in this role was Clifton Down which often was the destination for special trains used by passengers travelling to Bristol Zoo (the Monkey Specials) or to shows on the Downs. Clifton Bridge station also fulfilled this role with exhibitions at Ashton Meadows, whilst the nearby Ashton Gate was first opened to serve football crowds travelling to and from Bristol City's ground at Ashton Gate. Stapleton Road also had a role in this respect when Eastville was the home of Bristol Rovers F.C.

Many of the suburban stations in Bristol were also the departure points for holiday makers and day trippers to destinations throughout England and Wales. In many cases the excursion trains actually started from the suburban stations, Clifton Down being a favourite departure point. Lawrence Hill, Stapleton Road, Fishponds, Brislington, Bedminster and Parson Street were also important, whilst Ashley Hill was a starting point for many children's excursions from the nearby Muller's Orphanage and local schools.

A further role for both Temple Meads and a number of suburban stations, in particular Lawrence Hill and Stapleton Road, was as the departure point for evacuees leaving the city during the early days of the Second World War. Apart from movements to and from work, relatively little traffic was generated between the suburban stations within the city. Commuter traffic to and from the city centre has never reached a great volume compared with many other cities, no doubt because of the distance of Temple Meads station from the city centre employment focus. St Philips station was better placed for this, but only received a limited service. The whole picture could have been so different if the plans to develop a more central station in the mid-1860s had come to fruition.

Bristol Temple Meads

OPENED: 31st August 1840 (with the opening of the Bristol – Bath section of the GWR Bristol – London (Paddington) line).

CLOSED: Passengers – remains open for passenger services to and from London, the midlands, the north, South Wales, the south coast and west country.
Goods – 1982.

The focus of the rail network in Bristol has always been at Temple Meads. The well-known Bristol historian Bryan Little noted: 'All architecture expresses history – political, personal, social or financial. This is as true of early railway stations as it is of castles, cathedrals, towns or stately homes. Of no railway building is this more certain than Temple Meads at Bristol. The station's very name looks back to the twelfth century. Its structure and evolution reflect the transport history of the West of England and of at least four railway companies, whose trains used this uniquely historic complex of tracks, platforms and offices'. Bristol Temple Meads is the largest group of Grade I listed railway buildings in Britain.

From the early conception of the Bristol to London railway it was clear that the Bristol terminus would have to be located in one of the few level and open expanses of land that remained close to the city centre. The chosen location, some three quarters of a mile south east of the city centre, was low lying land just outside the line of the medieval town wall and enclosed by a loop of the River Avon, an area long known as Temple Meadows or Meads. To bring the railway further into the city centre would, even at that time, have been very expensive as much of the land was by then already developed with housing and industry. In 1835, at the passing of the Great Western Railway Act, most of the chosen site was still open ground bounded at its western edge by the main road from Bristol to Bath. It is surprising that the site was still undeveloped in the late 1830s: Brunel's view was that it was the only suitable site available.

A key factor in the development of the station was that the Floating Harbour, adjacent to the site, was still used for ship movements. Any railway line crossing the low-lying marshes had to allow for the navigational rights of sailing barges and thus the new terminus and the railway had to be at least 15 ft above ground level. Most of the 20-acre station site was bought from the Corporation of Bristol in 1836 for £12,000; however final portions of the site were not acquired from other owners until early 1839. During that year final discussions took place on the design of the main station buildings though work was already in hand on some railway facilities. Brunel's first designs of the terminal buildings were a great deal more ambitious than those finally built, the final scheme being a compromise between Brunel's ambitions and economic concerns of the GWR directors.

Preparatory work commenced in July 1839 but major construction started early in 1840; this date is recorded by the Roman numerals MDCCCXL cut on a scroll in stone above the side doorway to the offices and boardroom. Building work was actually completed in 1841 probably in time for the opening of the through line to London in June of that year. However, passenger trains commenced from the unfinished building running to Bath on 31st August 1840. By that date it is believed that the main booking hall and departure platform had been completed. It is perhaps surprising that no special ceremony beyond the flying of flags and ringing of church bells marked this public opening of the line. The first train, advertised to start from the unfinished terminus at 8 a.m., departed only a few minutes late, although it is recorded that the last rail into the terminus station had not been well and truly laid until half an hour previously. The first train drawn by 'Fireball', gaily decorated with flags, was made up of three First Class and five Second Class carriages filled by the general public who had previously obtained tickets in the large booking hall downstairs in the terminus.

The original Brunel terminus, as noted earlier, was constructed some 15 ft above ground level, this height being required not only because of navigational rights on the Floating Harbour, but also because the actual site sloped down from east to west. The external dimensions of the terminus were some 408 ft by 114 ft. Brunel overcame the height problems by building a series of semi-circular brick arched vaults; some say that this was done with cellarage in mind though in the early days some vaults were used for stabling railway horses. Upon this vaulted structure he laid the tracks and built the magnificent terminus station.

The station was broadly in three distinct parts. First, at the eastern end, was the spectacular main Train Shed wide enough to accommodate five broad gauge tracks. With walls of local limestone, it had a spectacular timber cantilevered glazed roof some 220 ft in length and with a span of 72 ft unsupported by any cross tie or abutment. When constructed it was the widest timber roof in Britain, greater even than Westminster Hall. This mock hammerbeam roof is carried on an arcade of timber arches supported by octagonal iron columns. Spaced 10 ft apart these were initially rather close (3ft 6 inches) to the edge of the platforms and created an awkward obstruction for passengers and gave little clearance when carriage doors opened. This problem continued until the broad gauge tracks were removed with the introduction of the standard gauge, the opportunity being taken at that stage for the platforms to be widened. The platforms extended 200 ft east into the open beyond the Train Shed. On each side of the Train Shed were smaller structures used for various purposes. On the northern departure side were the booking offices and waiting rooms (gents and ladies) behind the impressive main station entrance which for some years had a small canopy; passengers climbed stairs to the departure platform but bulky luggage could be conveyed by a lift. No refreshment facilities were provided.

The main Train Shed led westwards into the second section of the terminus building known as the Engine and Carriage Shed. Here engines came to rest and were stored or moved across by a traverser to other lines. This somewhat dingy and inferior section had a low flat ceiling supported by closely spaced plain iron columns. Above this Engine and Carriage Shed were draughtsmen's offices and other work places, all beneath the main roofline continuing from the Train Shed. It is said that at times smoke and steam from the engines filtered up through the floor boards into the draughtsmen's offices reminding them vividly of the activities for which they were drawing!

The final element in the Bristol terminus, with its frontage at an angle to the alignment of the tracks, was the original main GWR boardroom and offices fronting on to Bath Parade, now Temple Gate. This magnificent building, 184 ft in length and designed to reflect the status of the prestigious GWR, also originally incorporated the residence of the station superintendent. The angle of the frontage is such that the southern section of the building is somewhat narrower than the northern. The symmetrical Tudor/Gothic style frontage of this three-storey terminus building had angle turrets and a central two-storey oriel window above which were the coats of arms of the cities of Bristol and London, adopted by the GWR as its own arms. The Bath Parade facade was of a classical design; the only slight jarring feature was the large tall water tower supplying the engines which projected above the building at its southern end. In the 1860s the pavement level in front of the

Bristol Temple Meads. An engraving by J. Harris of the south east side of Brunel's station in about 1842. The GWR main offices (left) front on to Bath Parade (now Temple Gate). The full length of the Engine and Carriage Shed and Train Shed are shown. A horse bus emerges from the arrival gateway.

building was raised and a wooden fence erected; at a later date this was replaced by ornate iron railings incorporating a gate and with steps leading to an imposing doorway. Originally there were two flanking gateways, that on the left as you faced the building (the departure side) having a clock. This led to the appropriately named cobbled Clock Tower Yard (in early days called the 'Court of Departure'). The other gateway was surmounted by the Royal arms. The left hand archway gave access to the main passenger entrance and the booking offices on the departure (up) side of the Train Shed. Passengers arriving on trains left the terminus through the down side or right hand archway, passing through the original 'Court of Arrival'. These departure and arrival yards (originally Courts) on the north and south sides of the Train Shed were connected by a north-to-south passage through which road vehicles could pass, in the early days horses and carriages. The right gateway was later removed; the date for this removal was at one time linked to the electrification of the tramway terminus that had been developed in the 1890s on the south side of the building but all recent research indicates that its demolition came with the construction of the inclined road approach to the 1870s redeveloped station (see below).

In the main building facing on to Bath Parade various offices dealt with the operation of the railway including the main boardroom. Brunel designed a splendid staircase, wide and well lit, to reach this important room which had two fireplaces, one at each end. Company business was directed from this office until 1855 when the new station at Paddington opened and the GWR boardroom transferred to London.

Before moving on to consider further developments at Temple Meads two comments are worth quoting: David Atwell in his book *Railway Architecture* describes Brunel's original train terminus as 'without any parallel elsewhere in early railway architecture'. Colin Maggs in his book *Rail Centres – Bristol* notes, 'The whole impression of the original station was that of a gentleman's country seat and would have boosted the confidence of nervous early travellers'.

The first goods shed, a large building 326 ft long and 138 ft wide, was constructed to the north east of the passenger station on level ground beside the Floating Harbour, 12 ft below the main railway and at right angles to it. Access was provided by turntables and a double lift resembling a large pair of scales worked by hydraulic power whereby trucks were alternately raised and lowered. This early goods shed, with a capacity of 209 wagons and equipped with cranes, was finished in the autumn of 1842 and also handled the Bristol and Exeter Railway Company's goods traffic until 1850 when that company opened its own depot at Pylle Hill, west of Temple Meads on 1st May. This early depot proved inadequate for the ever-increasing goods traffic and over the period 1874-76 it was completely remodelled by Rowland Brotherhood, the Chippenham contractor. An old dock on the Floating Harbour was filled in and replaced by a wharf with steam and hydraulic cranes; a 1 in 60 ramp was also constructed giving direct rail access replacing the old lift which had caused great delays. The goods yard was raised 3 ft 6 inches and a new goods shed constructed some 445 ft long, accommodating 200 wagons; there was space for a further 232 wagons in

An early engraving showing detail of the Bath Parade frontage. The departure gateway (left) leads to the Clock Tower yard. The arrival gateway (right) was demolished with the construction of the new incline, during the 1870s major redevelopment.

An early close-up of the imposing Bath Parade frontage of the Brunel offices. Note the fine detail of the facade and the iron railings that for some years stretched across the building beside the pavement. To the right is the arrival gateway demolished with the construction of the new incline to the 1870s extension.

the outside yard. Once again this proved inadequate and in 1924 an even larger depot was built at a cost of £556,450. Within the five acre site the covered shed was apparently at that time the largest covered area in Britain. Under the one roof there were 15 platforms, each 575 ft long and 30 ft wide; 408 wagons could be accommodated in the shed and a further 330 were able to stand in the yard. All the latest electric technology was incorporated in the yard which remained operational until the late 1970s. Even with the modern equipment horses were apparently used for deliveries until 1952 and for shunting until 1962. In its last years the goods shed was used by National Carriers; it finally closed on 1st August 1982 and was demolished in May 1983.

When the Bristol and Exeter Railway opened the first stage of its line as far as Bridgwater in 1841 it used the GWR Brunel terminus at Bristol. This involved the inconvenient, time consuming, reversal of trains into and out of the station. However, in 1845, in accordance with a scheme agreed in 1839, the B&ER opened its own terminus at right angles to the east end of the GWR station. With

hindsight it is remarkable, bearing in mind the B&ER had been authorised in 1836, that Brunel, engineer to both the GWR and B&ER, did not take the opportunity to establish a single joint station to serve both companies. The fact that the GWR and B&ER were distinct companies at that stage was clearly the decisive factor. The B&ER station was a single-storey simple wooden construction on brick vaults, with an overall roof that lacked the height of the nearby GWR terminus. One writer described it as resembling some of the single-storey sheds built alongside the quays in the Bristol City Docks. Another referred to it as a 'simple makeshift structure'. It spanned two platform tracks and also three centre tracks for stabling coaches. Because of its construction and position near the Cattle Market, it soon became known as the 'Cow Shed'. An access road was provided from Bath Parade separate from that to the GWR terminus. A double track curve linked the two railways and an 'express platform' was also provided in 1845 by the Bristol and Exeter on the up line, close to its own terminus; this was used by both up and down through expresses. The express platform was not used by all expresses as in

A fine overall view in May 1872. Illustrated are Brunel's 1840/41 Train Shed (right), the 1845 Bristol and Exeter station (top left) and the magnificent Bristol and Exeter offices (top). Most tracks are of mixed gauge with a number of carriage/wagon turntables to transfer rolling stock between them. Note the road carriage on a flat wagon (middle left).

1862 it is recorded that the down Flying Dutchman train to the west country ran to the end of the curve and backed into the Bristol and Exeter terminus itself.

Initiatives were taken by the Bristol and Exeter Railway to improve facilities at this under-provided station. Late in 1851 tenders were submitted for a new booking office and £1,100 was spent on providing this facility. Four months later new furniture was bought for the waiting room and for the refreshment room which opened in 1852; an amenity that was lacking in the Great Western station. The express platform was also extended and given a roof in that year.

In 1852 the Bristol and Exeter Railway commenced work on the building which is its best remaining contribution to the railway complex at Temple Meads. This was its headquarters offices to a design chosen as the result of a competition. The winning design, of Jacobean style, was submitted by Samuel C. Fripp, a local architect already known for previous work at Temple Meads. To allow for possible flooding and also to compensate for the light excluding effect of the ramp sloping up from

Bath Parade to the B&ER station itself, the lowest floor was 10 ft above ground level and was entered by a doorway of a Jacobean Renaissance type with the arms of the Bristol and Exeter Company incorporated. The whole building is of symmetrical Jacobean design with shaped gables and twin towers and, built around a central atrium, was completed in October 1854 at a cost of £6,600. When the Bristol and Exeter Company amalgamated with the Great Western Railway in 1876 these offices were taken over by the GWR Bristol Traffic Division. They remain in use today (see below).

From 1844 services to and from the Midlands and Gloucester, operated by the Bristol and Gloucester Railway (later Midland Railway), began to use the Brunel GWR station. Large increases in both passenger and goods traffic followed in the 1850s and 1860s. The latter included the opening of the Bristol and South Wales Union Railway in 1863. Urgent action was needed to relieve the congestion at the old Brunel terminus and the inadequate Bristol and Exeter station. Late in the spring of 1861 the Great Western Railway Board received a deputation from the Bristol Chamber of Commerce. This sought the co-operation of the Great Western and other railways in the promotion of a scheme whereby the line at Temple Meads could be extended to the City Docks and Queen Square where a central station would be built. This proposal was unfortunately, as it later turned out, rejected by a narrow majority of the City Council so the Bristol and Exeter, Midland and Great Western Railway Companies resorted to the idea of building a new joint station at Temple Meads itself. It was clearly necessary as in 1863 only two platforms in the original Brunel terminus dealt with GWR trains running to London, Westbury and New Passage Pier (for South Wales) and Midland Railway services to Birmingham. An edition of the *Bristol Times and Mirror* commented, 'It will be difficult to find in all England a more rambling, ill-arranged and melancholy looking group of buildings than those for the Midland, Great Western and Bristol and Exeter lines. The Midland and Great Western Brunel station makes a massive show outside; but the outside is delusive for the accommodation provided by way of offices is of the smallest. It is really a punishment for a man to have to squeeze himself in among the crowd that assembles every day at the starting of every train, in front of a single pigeon hole that is used for the issue of tickets and for a lady, the difficulty of getting a ticket must be something dreadful. The Bristol and Exeter is certainly a trifle better in this respect than the others but not much.'

On 19th June 1865 the GWR, B&ER and MR obtained an Act to build a new joint station but because of disputes regarding the proportionate division of the cost, another six years elapsed before work began and a further six were needed for the task to be completed. The final agreed costs were shared GWR 3/8, MR 3/8 and B&ER 2/8. Another problem faced was that of the road link from the Temple Meads location to Bristol Bridge and the historic centre of the city. In 1865 a proposal was made to construct a new street, fundamentally the same scheme as one recommended some 20 years earlier. This time the project was approved and completed in 1871 with the new thoroughfare, Victoria Street, linking the city centre direct to the joint station. Links with the city centre were also enhanced with the inauguration of a horse tram service between Bristol Bridge and Bath Bridge in April 1879; this service was extended to Three Lamps, Totterdown, in November of the same year. In 1881 the service was again extended, this time from Bristol Bridge to the Drawbridge (St Augustine's Reach) using the 'new' Baldwin Street. Some of the horse-drawn services commenced or terminated at Temple Meads Station and a covered shed was constructed in the space between the original

Viewed from the west the fine curved Train Shed under construction in August 1876. The two principal through platforms and the down side narrow island platform (centre right) are already in place.

18

The south-west end of the 1870s curved Train Shed in the early 1900s. A train stands at the 1892 extension of the main down platform. The additional narrow up side island platform, inserted under the roof in 1899, can also be seen (centre left).

An aerial view in the 1920s. Across the centre of the picture from left to right is the original 1840s Brunel station and the 1870s Digby Wyatt extension. The 1870s curved Train Shed is featured, of particular interest is the down side entrance/exit (centre extreme right) lost in the 1930s major extensions. Also prominent are the huge goods depot (centre top) and the 1854 Bristol and Exeter offices (centre bottom).

A fine view of the 1870s incline dated 1915. Very prominent is the Bristol Tramways station inserted between the left hand side of the incline and the Brunel station Engine and Carriage Shed. Early motor taxis are busy particularly on the 'way out' carriageway.

A close-up of the central office block and clock tower soon after its completion in the 1870s. Note the intricate detail of the main building, the tall 'spire' rising above the clock tower and the fine canopies. Horse-drawn carriages wait for passengers.

Brunel Engine and Carriage Shed and the 1870s incline. The Tram Shed included stables. With the electrification of the route via Temple Meads in 1899 the covered shed was developed into a tramway station including a ticket office and passenger waiting facilities. After the trams ceased at the outset of the Second World War, a section of the site was used by a railway workers' canteen. Sections of the old tramlines were left and can still be seen today.

In 1871 work commenced on the new joint station. The Bristol and Exeter terminus was demolished and a great curved iron and glass roofed train shed with a span of 125 ft was built over the site of the former Bristol and Exeter express platform. Some 500 ft long the curved shed covered two outer platforms and a narrow island platform on the down side (i.e. there were four platform faces). Also under the roof were further through tracks for rolling stock storage. All tracks were of broad gauge. To the north of the new curved train shed Brunel's original station was lengthened eastwards in a similar style to the original, although the roof supports in the new section were wrought iron tie bars in marked contrast to Brunel's wooden arches. The platforms with this eastern extension were 352 yds long compared with the original 140 yds. The focus of the new station was an imposing 100 ft stone building within the apex between the extended Brunel train shed and the new curved shed. The ornamental stone turreted facade in perpendicular Gothic style perpetuated Brunel's original architectural concept;

the building was surmounted by a clock tower and a steeply pitched wooden 'spire'. Built generally of Draycott (Somerset) stone, it formed an impressive frontage to the rebuilt station. In this new building each company had its own booking office within the high cathedral-like entrance hall. Passengers for the respective companies entered by separate doors, a scroll above each bearing the appropriate legend, Midland Railway over the left hand door, Bristol and Exeter Railway over the centre and Great Western Railway over the right. Inside the entrance doors were pinewood porters' booths, which are still in place. The original pine entrance doors were later removed; they often had to be left open and this caused the entrance hall to be cold and draughty in winter. They were replaced by glass swing doors. The central building also incorporated refreshment and waiting rooms, a telegraph office and parcels office.

The new station forecourt in front of the stone building was accessed by a new wide inclined approach road up from the main Bath Road which now brought passengers to platform level. As noted earlier the construction of this enhanced access was instrumental in the demolition of the original Brunel right-hand arch. Access to the down platforms was by a road running past the Bristol and Exeter offices, passing under the tracks, south west of the station.

The completed and revamped enlarged station was formally opened on 1st January 1878 though sections had come into use earlier. The major

A striking view looking west under the curved Train Shed roof in about 1906. Taken from the east end of the main up platform, the two narrow island platforms and the main down platform (extreme left) are connected by a long footbridge. Various types of trolley stand on the platforms and an engine enters from the west on one of the two tracks between the island platforms.

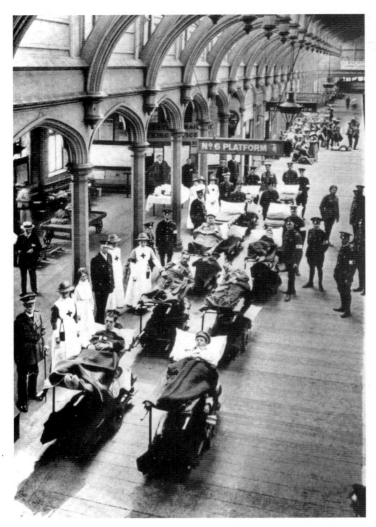

A scene in the original Brunel Train Shed in about 1916. During the Great War many hospital trains arrived at the station. Red Cross nurses tend the wounded on the double decker stretchers before they are transferred to local hospitals.

The Black Watch Regiment marching up the incline on 21st April 1915. The Bristol Tramways station for its electric trams is prominent in the centre of the picture.

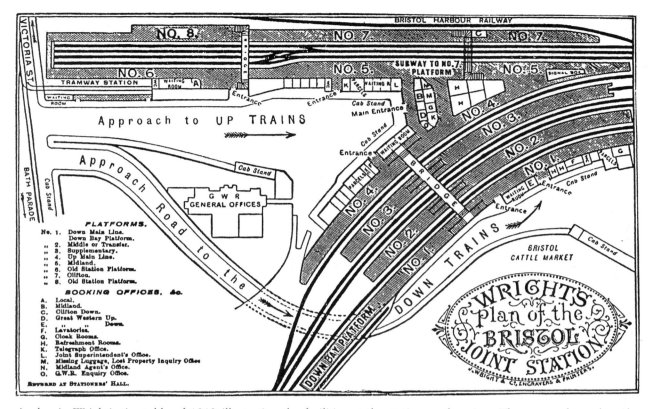

A plan in Wright's timetable of 1912 illustrating the facilities at the station at that time. The approach road to the down side was lost during the rebuilding of the early 1930s. Platform 3 was added in 1899 and the down platform bay in 1892.

restructuring was undertaken to the overall designs of Brunel's former architectural associate Sir Matthew Digby Wyatt. The detailed design of the wrought iron structure was the work of Francis Fox, the Bristol and Exeter Railway engineer. He was also responsible for the detailed design of the intricate green and gold exterior canopy which was added after completion of other work and is virtually identical to the one he designed for the Weston-super-Mare station opened in 1884. The main constructor of the 1870s rebuilding was Vernon & Evans of Cheltenham.

Even before its completion, however, the new joint station was considered inadequate and several minor accidents between 1871 and 1876 were attributed by the Board of Trade inspectors directly or indirectly to the congested state of the new station. One report of 1876, two years before its official completion, indeed asserted that 'the station is clearly much less than adequate for the amount of traffic to be handled'. In 1892 a down bay platform was added and seven years later, in January 1899, an additional narrow island platform was constructed on the up side under the new curved train shed, this made possible in the space created by the conversion of the broad gauge to standard gauge in May 1892. A footbridge connected the now four platforms. In 1902 a wooden footbridge was built in the Brunel terminal station spoiling the vista of the splendid roof, but this was removed and replaced by a pedestrian and baggage subway in the 1930s general rebuilding of the Temple Meads complex. The details of the station facilities in 1912 are shown in the plan reproduced from a local timetable.

In 1914 the Great Western Railway decided to remodel the permanent way and extend the station but the outbreak of the First World War prevented these plans going ahead. By the 1920s the situation was reaching crisis point and in the summer there was major congestion on the lines around Bristol as trains attempted to come into Temple Meads station. The railway companies themselves could not be entirely blamed for this state of affairs as the only room for extension of the station was over Bristol Corporation's Cattle Market and to this the City Council raised continual objections. The only immediate post-First World War improvement was doubling the width of the footbridge

23

Sir Robert Baden Powell leading a scout parade away from the rarely photographed pre-1930s south east entrance/ exit en route to a local jamboree in about 1920.

spanning the platforms of the through station and providing a new exit from it directly on to the approach road. This work was completed on 10th July 1920.

In 1929 as a measure to assist easing unemployment during the depression, the Government made loans available to carry out large public works and it was agreed that an enlargement of Temple Meads station would qualify. Work commenced, under the direction of P.E. Culverhouse, to enlarge the station to more than twice its size. Major widening of the bridges over the Floating Harbour and the River Avon enabled platform lengthening whilst the purchase of extra land allowed the addition of the two outer island platforms. The number of platforms increased from nine to 15, a considerable proportion of this extension being on the site of the adjoining cattle market. The longest platform, numbers 9 and 10 combined, the tenth longest in the country, was 1,366 ft in length, compared with the previous longest platform of 920 ft. It was estimated that the length of all the platforms at the new Temple Meads station totalled some two miles (10,487 ft), the station now covering an area of fifteen acres. As a part of this reconstruction the two narrow island platforms under the train shed were removed allowing the two side main platforms to be widened significantly.

Work commenced in November 1930 with the firm Shanks & McEwan of Glasgow being the main contractors. The canopies over the new platforms were of an umbrella or arcade type supported by columns rather than an expensive overall train shed, while the buildings were constructed of cream and terracotta bricks and glazed tiling on a grey granite plinth (similar materials were used at other GWR stations reconstructed at that time, for example at Cardiff Central). The widened through platforms under the train shed were opened on 25th March 1935, after more than two years reconstruction. Two new island platforms to the south on the former cattle market site had been brought into use over a year earlier on 26th February 1934. The completed new station had five up and five down through platforms, a bay for Portishead line trains and four platforms in the old Brunel terminus. With this reconstruction all main platforms were provided with refreshment and waiting rooms. The booking office, given a modern cast iron and bronze front, was set back to give a spacious circulating area.

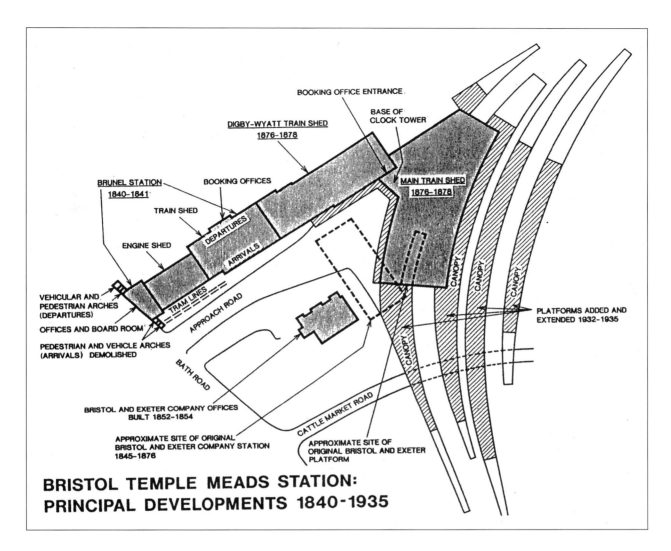

BOOKING OFFICE ENTRANCE

DIGBY-WYATT TRAIN SHED
1876-1878

BASE OF
CLOCK TOWER

BRUNEL STATION
1840-1841

BOOKING OFFICES

MAIN TRAIN SHED
1876-1878

TRAIN SHED

DEPARTURES

ENGINE SHED

ARRIVALS

CANOPY

CANOPY

CANOPY

VEHICULAR AND
PEDESTRIAN ARCHES
(DEPARTURES)

TRAM LINES

APPROACH ROAD

CANOPY

PLATFORMS ADDED AND
EXTENDED 1932-1935

OFFICES AND BOARD ROOM

PEDESTRIAN AND VEHICLE ARCHES
(ARRIVALS) DEMOLISHED

BATH ROAD

BRISTOL AND EXETER COMPANY OFFICES
BUILT 1852-1854

CATTLE MARKET ROAD

APPROXIMATE SITE OF ORIGINAL
BRISTOL AND EXETER COMPANY STATION
1845-1876

APPROXIMATE SITE OF
ORIGINAL BRISTOL AND EXETER
PLATFORM

**BRISTOL TEMPLE MEADS STATION:
PRINCIPAL DEVELOPMENTS 1840-1935**

Passengers now reached their platforms by a 300 ft long, 30 ft wide subway which replaced the footbridge; this also gave access to hairdressing salons, toilets and baths. Parcels were carried in electric trolleys along a special subway, connecting the parcels depot with all platforms. Electric lifts connected platforms with the subway but rather surprisingly gas lighting was used for the new platforms and indeed remained in use until 1960 when replaced by fluorescent electric lighting. The new enlarged Temple Meads station was finally completed in December 1935.

During the early days of the Second World War, Bristol Temple Meads was a prime target as a key traffic centre. In the first six months it received little damage but on 2nd December 1940 the station was hit and various suburban lines put out of action for several hours. Four days later there were heavy casualties on the 7.10 p.m. to Salisbury which received a direct hit at the station. On 3rd January 1941 the station was hit by incendiary bombs. All were thought to have been extinguished but one lodged behind the clock and started a fire which destroyed the tower's wooden spire and burned out the telegraph office and telephone exchange above the booking office; the last was badly damaged by water. Tickets were soon available, however, at Army huts erected in the station approach. During the Second World War, Bristol was an important centre for both goods traffic and military personnel, wartime traffic often being hectic. Tunnels below the station were used as an emergency centre for key railwaymen and as an air raid shelter for passengers and staff. Many evacuees from Bristol departed from Temple Meads. In both World Wars, injured servicemen were brought to the station before being transferred by ambulance to hospitals in the Bristol area.

THEN A fine view of the central offices and clock tower decorated for the centenary of the GWR in 1935. The fine detail of the buildings and the clock tower spire are well illustrated.

NOW A similar view 70 years later on 23rd May 2005. The clock tower 'spire' has gone, destroyed 64 years before in the air-raid of 3rd January 1941 (see photo opposite). The cars in the forecourt are of a different era!

Looking west in the main Train Shed in October 1934 during the major rebuilding. The large hut (right) stands on what is now Platform 3 which is being widened as part of the reconstruction. The former island platforms and footbridge had been demolished before the photo was taken.

The station forecourt shortly after the air-raid of 3rd January 1941 in which incendiary bombs caused extensive damage including the loss of the tall 'spire' on the clock tower.

With the reduction in rail passenger traffic in the 1960s the platforms in the original Brunel train shed became redundant. This section of the station was closed to all rail traffic on 12th September 1965 and became a car park from February 1966. The new MAS signal box was unfortunately built blocking future rail access to the old Brunel Train Shed and the Digby Wyatt extension. In February 1981 the original Brunel buildings were rescued from dereliction by the Brunel Engineering Trust which took a 99 year lease from British Rail with the aim of undertaking a comprehensive restoration programme. Unfortunately the Trust was unable to complete the work, although much restoration was undertaken. In 1989 the British Empire and Commonwealth Museum Trust acquired the lease and from this time work on the fabric progressed with guidance and support from English Heritage and the Railway Heritage Trust. For some years the Exploratory, a hands-on science project, was based in the building. The British and Empire Commonwealth Museum has become a major visitor attraction; in the original Train Shed a new floor has been laid filling the space between the two former platforms and the large space is now used for a variety of major events including antiques fairs, fashion shows and art exhibitions.

Adjacent to the museum entrance, in the forecourt on the north side of the station incline, sections of the old tramlines remain in place. In mid-2005 a children's nursery Buffer Bear occupied a part of the vaulted area next to the museum entrance with play equipment laid out alongside the rising station incline.

In 1985 Temple Meads was honoured by a visit from Her Majesty Queen Elizabeth II who inspected restoration work in the Brunel buildings when visiting an exhibition setting out the 150 year history of the Great Western Railway. For the first time the Royal Standard flew at Temple Meads; on previous visits the Sovereign was only passing through the station and flying the Standard was not appropriate.

The Digby Wyatt eastern extension of the original Brunel building is used today as the undercover section of the station pay-and-display car park. Since the early 1990s a number of major restoration initiatives have been undertaken on the now operational parts of the station. In 1990/1991 some £2 million was spent on a major restoration of the iron and glass roof of the curved train shed. Also completed at that time was a clean up of the Temple Gate frontage of the Brunel terminus. Between August 1998 and the end of

The coronation of Queen Elizabeth II is celebrated at the station in this view of 1953.

THEN An atmospheric photograph of 22nd May 1956, some 10 years before this area ceased to be used for rail operations. In the foreground is the west section of the 1870s Digby Wyatt extension including the signal box, in use until 12th September 1965. Beyond is the Train Shed section of the original Brunel station and in the distance the low Engine and Carriage Shed.

NOW The former Train Shed section with the area between the two former platforms now filled in, photographed on 23rd May 2005 with preparatory work in progress for a major art exhibition. The 1870s Digby Wyatt section behind the photographer is used for car parking, the former signal box being still in situ.

1999 some £7 million was spent on renovation of those sections of the station complex dating back to the 1870s and 1930s. This included renovation of the main frontage and clock tower, paving and resurfacing of the platforms and booking hall, refurbishment of the platform canopies and further repairs to the main train shed roof. Reacting to the growing pressure on platform availability, the former outer island platform, which had been out of use for some years, was refurbished and brought back into use in 2001 as platforms 13 and 15.

The 1852 Bristol and Exeter office building remains intact, fittingly now called Bristol and Exeter House; a plaque inside the main entrance records that the name was given on 1st November 1982 by L. Lloyd, the then general manager of British Rail Western Region. In spring 2005 the building was in partial railway office use but further office space was indicated as being available to let. Opposite the main entrance space under the station approach incline was at that time in various commercial uses in 'Bristol and Exeter Mews'.

The north west side of the former Brunel station in July 1998 following major restoration work. The former Engine and Carriage Shed is on the right with the slightly wider Train Shed to the left, the principal entrance being beneath the twin turrets (left). The vehicle passageway between the departure and arrival courtyards can be seen in the centre of the picture.

The south east side of the former Brunel Engine and Carriage Shed on 27th October 2001. In the centre is the entrance to the British Empire and Commonwealth Museum; to the bottom right a children's nursery operates.

The Suburban Stations and Halts

Ashley Hill

OPENED: 13th August 1864 (on the Bristol – South Wales line originally opened through this site in 1863).

CLOSED: Passengers – 23rd November 1964. Goods – 1st November 1966.

Ashley Hill, when opened in August 1864, was a small station with one platform on the single track Bristol to South Wales line which ran from Bristol Temple Meads north through the developing suburbs and countryside to the banks of the Severn Estuary at New Passage. The line, built by the Bristol and South Wales Union Railway, had been ceremonially opened almost a year earlier, on 25th August 1863 and opened to the public on 8th September 1863. Doubling of the line and the addition of a second platform at Ashley Hill came in 1885 in readiness for the opening of the Severn Tunnel in 1886. The principal station building was sited on the down (Ashley Down) side of the double track; a particular feature in the early 1900s was the very attractive station garden on each platform.

The station was rebuilt in the early 1930s when the line to South Wales through Ashley Hill was quadrupled, the re-opening taking place on 30th April 1933. The earlier building on the down platform was retained in the new layout. At this time Ashley Hill had a particularly good service with local trains running on the circuit through Pilning, Severn Beach, Avonmouth and Clifton. For some years the station acted as a departure point for excursions of local children, a particular feature being those organised by the nearby Muller's Orphanage. In the 1930s, after redevelopment, an average of eight to 10 men were employed at the station itself and in the six siding goods yard which

A rail motor arrives at the up platform. The principal building with a fine canopy is on the down platform (left), the original signal box stands at the north end.

Looking north in about 1910. A train approaches the up platform of the pre-1930s station on the then double track. Note the rural setting – Lockleaze had not yet developed and Muller Road had not been constructed.

The station garden on the down platform in 1904 advertising 'Express GWR Services'. Top right is the Ashley Hill Station Hotel, now in residential use.

THEN A later view north this time showing the 1930s rebuilt station on the now four track line. Note the earlier building retained on the down platform (left).

NOW Looking north on 14th March 2005. Note the remnants of the down platform edge (foreground). The 1458 Bristol Temple Meads to Newcastle Virgin Voyager is halted by signals at the site of the northern end of the 1933 station.

A party of girls from the nearby Muller's Orphanage pose before an outing in front of the shelter on the up platform of the pre-1930s Ashley Hill station.

had opened on 4th August 1925 on the down side north of the station. A 33-lever signal box operated just south of the goods yard entrance from 5th July 1925 to 19th October 1970.

Ashley Hill closed to passenger traffic in November 1964 and to goods two years later. The number of tracks through the station site was reduced from four to two as from 2nd February 1984. Today the principal remains are sections of the platform and railings on the down side, together with a subway taking a public footpath under the north end of the former station site. Some rubble can be seen at the site of the former main building. The bank behind the former down platform, once laid out as an attractive garden, is now a wilderness of small trees and undergrowth. The former Station Hotel at the corner of Station Road and Lilstock Avenue remains, now in private residential use.

Ashton Gate

OPENED: 15th September 1906 (football supporters), 1st October 1906 (general public) (on the Portishead branch originally opened through this site in 1867).

CLOSED: 1st November 1917.

RE-OPENED: 23rd May 1926.

CLOSED: 7th September 1964.

Subsequent temporary uses 1970-1977 for football specials and May 1984 for 'Mission England' at Ashton Gate Stadium.

The impetus for the construction of this station was the promotion of Bristol City Football Club into the Football League First Division. Rapid construction of a simple wooden structure took place and Ashton Gate Platform opened for football supporters on 15th September 1906. A service for other passengers commenced some two weeks later on 1st October. The Platform closed eleven years later, in 1917, primarily as a wartime austerity measure, although a further factor was clearly that Bristol City were no longer in the First Division! A rebuilt Ashton Gate Platform reopened in May 1926, this time with the prime intention of encouraging passenger traffic on the Portishead line; in August 1928 the name changed to Ashton Gate in the timetable. However the name board remained unchanged as 'Platform'.

Throughout much of its life, Ashton Gate had its greatest use for football excursions. On many winter Saturdays three or four local trains came from within the Bristol area, for instance from Clifton Down and Avonmouth, and these were often augmented by large excursion trains from all parts of the country. It is recorded that on occasions Specials drawn by Pacific locomotives came from the Southern Region. The wide access path and footbridge assisted with the dispersal of large crowds. When the special trains had emptied their passengers they normally drew forward as far as Clifton Bridge station where the engine ran around the empty stock and

Looking north in 1963. Note the wide sloping access path (left) provided originally to accommodate large numbers of football supporters arriving for games at the nearby Bristol City F.C. stadium.

35

THEN A special train from Oxford has arrived at the refurbished original down platform on 12th May 1984 bringing passengers to the Billy Graham 'Mission England' meeting at the nearby Ashton Gate stadium.

NOW About 21 years later, on 14th May 2005, the remnants of both platforms are still visible. The line has been re-laid and reopened carrying freight trains to and from Royal Portbury Dock.

pulled it back towards Bristol. Storage of this stock normally took place in Ashton Meadows on the Canons Marsh freight line which had opened in 1906.

To cope with the major influx of passengers, signalmen on the Portishead branch were often recruited to work at Ashton Gate on Saturday afternoon, collecting tickets and closing carriage doors. Many of these volunteers, having completed their work, moved off to the match. After the Second World War use by Football Specials first decreased and then stopped whilst regular passenger services ceased on the Portishead branch from 7th September 1964 and thus at Ashton Gate. Staffing ceased as from 29th October 1962, Ashton Gate being designated as a halt.

A temporary revival came with the use once again for Football Specials, the first excursion to arrive being a three car DMU special from Birmingham on 29th September 1970. The revival was short-lived though and it closed again in 1977 with Parson Street taking up the role of the arrival and departure point for football excursions with fans being escorted on the mile walk from the station. No excursions arrived at Ashton Gate during the period when Bristol City were in the First Division from 1976 to 1980. The down platform had been shortened at the southern end during road widening during 1975.

The final use came when the station was again reopened from 12th-19th May 1984 for special trains bringing passengers to the major Billy Graham 'Mission England' campaign being held at Ashton Gate football ground. For this event considerable temporary refurbishment took place. Today only remnants of the down platform remain; the track was re-laid through Ashton Gate for the reopening of the Portishead branch in late 2001 associated with the introduction of freight traffic serving Royal Portbury Dock from early 2002.

Avonmouth

OPENED: 6th March 1865 (as the northern terminus of the Bristol Port Railway and Pier line).

CLOSED: 1st October 1902 (general public), 15th May 1903 (workers' trains).

This first Avonmouth station opened in March 1865 as the terminus of the single track Bristol Port Railway and Pier line which ran from Hotwells station, beneath the Suspension Bridge, downstream parallel to the River Avon. At its opening the station site was bleak, being surrounded by palings in the middle of a rather deserted landscape. Facilities included a 265 ft platform on the west side of the double track into the station and a 200 ft platform on the east side. On the latter stood a booking office and this was connected by a path to the grounds of the adjacent Avonmouth Hotel. A gate in the station fence led to a 300ft long pier, though at the time of the station's opening the pontoon and floating bridge connecting to the pier had not been completed. The pier opened on 3rd June 1865. The west side platform of the station became disused at an early date.

The development and operation of this original Avonmouth terminus cannot really be separated from the Avonmouth Hotel and the pier. In 1864, with the anticipated construction of the pier and the railway, a company was formed with the object of building a hotel and pleasure gardens adjacent to the new rail terminus. The prospectus of the Avonmouth Hotel

The only known photograph, dated 8th March 1903, of the original terminus of the Bristol Port Railway and Pier Company. Much enlarged from a more general photograph of the area, the platform and building (top middle) are behind a wooden fence separating the passenger line to Avonmouth Dock station from the 1900 single track freight only line linking Avonmouth to Pilning.

Company Ltd appeared in March 1864, capital available being £10,000. The prospectus estimated that some 100,000 people would visit the pleasure gardens annually and pay an admission fee of 3d. It was noted that customers for the gardens would also come from the many steamers sailing from the centre of Bristol to the new pier.

The hotel project was implemented with the opening of the Avonmouth Hotel on Easter Sunday, 10th April 1865. The Pleasure Gardens, of some 10 acres, were soon completed: facilities included a large and well equipped concert hall and an ornamental lake surrounded by statues. Concerts were organised in the hall by Mr F.B. Girdlestone, General Manager of the new port. The first rail excursion to the Pleasure Gardens ran on 11th July 1866. Tea and shrimps at Avonmouth became a popular excursion. Fêtes were held at Easter and Whitsun and many thousands of Bristolians made the trip by rail and steamer. Despite the early successes, the Gardens never became financially viable and losses soon accumulated. A further destination for rail passengers was the nearby rifle ranges of the 1st Gloucestershire Rifle Volunteers Corps.

During the building of the Royal Edward Dock in the early 1900s, the Avonmouth Hotel accommodated engineers engaged upon the dock scheme. With the closure of the station in 1902 the hotel became isolated. In 1910 its name changed to the Continental Hotel reflecting the fact that it provided a temporary home for many emigrants from Europe en route to the USA and Canada via Avonmouth. During the First World War the hotel housed the Women's Army Auxiliary Corps. It was demolished in 1926 during the construction of the eastern arm of the Royal Edward Dock which had originally opened in 1908.

The development of the Royal Edward Dock itself led directly to the closure of this original Avonmouth station, the site being required during construction. The public service was withdrawn on 1st October 1902 but unadvertised trains for workers continued until 15th May 1903, the formal closure taking effect the following day. From that time services on the line were terminated at the Avonmouth Dock station, first opened in 1877.

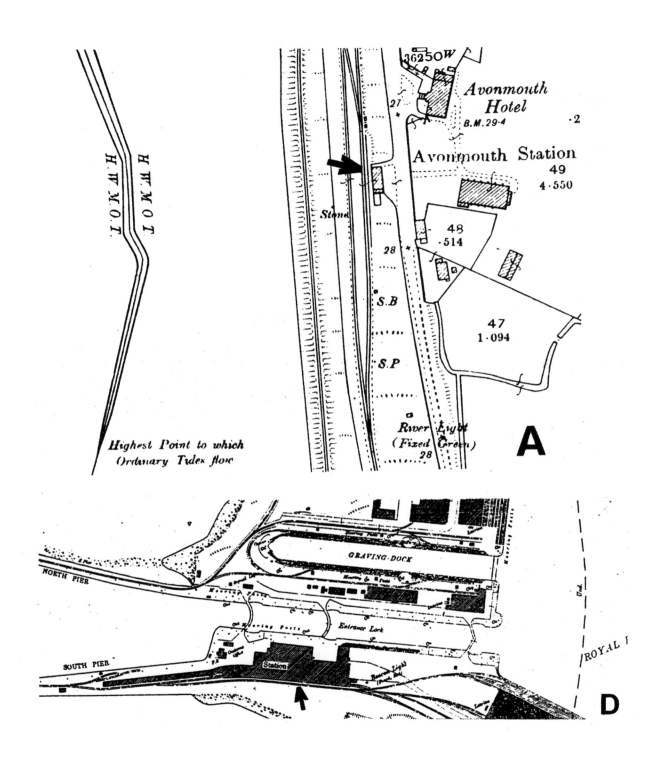

Avonmouth Stations. This series of maps shows the location of the various stations serving the Docks complex and housing at Avonmouth. Map A shows the first Avonmouth station close to the Avonmouth (later Continental) Hotel. Map B shows the Great Western and Midland Railway joint Avonmouth Dock station and the GWR Avonmouth Docks (GW) station at the east and west ends respectively of Gloucester Road which led to the main Docks gate. Map C shows the original facility for ships' passengers on the East Pier whilst Map D shows the new Royal Edward station on the South Pier, opened in 1910.

40

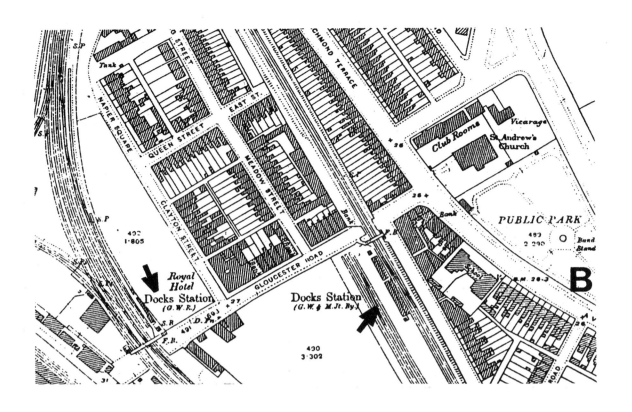

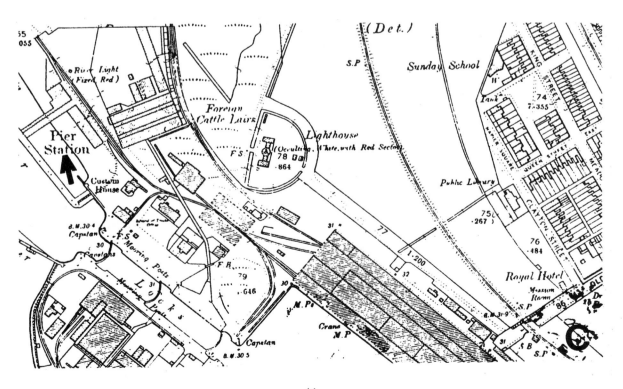

41

Avonmouth Dock

OPENED: c.1868 (workers' platform); 1877 (first station); 1st September 1885 (second station) (on the Hotwells – Avonmouth line originally opened through this site in 1865).

CLOSED: Passengers – remains open for services on the Bristol Temple Meads – Avonmouth – Severn Beach line. Goods – 20th June 1966.

Avonmouth Dock station, built at a cost of £275, opened in 1877 a little after the opening of the new Avonmouth Dock itself on 24th February that year. It was built at, or very close to, the site of an earlier platform erected in about 1868 on the Hotwells to Avonmouth line for use by dock construction workers. At the Dock's opening extra trains were run for spectators but these ran through to the original 1865 Avonmouth terminus and did not stop at the 1868 workers' platform on the south-west side of the then single track on account of its limited capacity.

With increasing traffic on a single track, the limited 1877 facilities were clearly inadequate and the Great Western and Midland Railways, the joint constructors of the Clifton Extension Railway that was about to link Avonmouth direct with Temple Meads, bought adjacent land near the Gloucester Road Dock gates for an expanded station and extra tracks. The new station, known as Avonmouth Dock Joint, opened on 1st September 1885. It comprised an island platform with one face for through traffic and the other a terminal line; on the island stood two wooden buildings with sloping canopies. The opening coincided with the commencement of passenger traffic on the direct line to Temple Meads via the new Clifton Down tunnel. Facilities were continually improved with increased passenger traffic to the developing port. In 1900 a new canopy and urinal were provided (total cost £250); in 1902 further improvements cost £80 whilst in August 1904 enlargements to the buildings and extensions to the platform cost £1,570. In the terminal bay a run-round loop was introduced in 1904 and was

Avonmouth Dock. The 1885 station looking north west in about 1913. An up platform was added to the right of the train adjacent to Portview Road in 1918 and the whole station was rebuilt in 1926.

well used through to the closure of the bay in 1966. Facilities were also provided to attract and handle new freight traffic. From 1st January 1904 separate goods staff were appointed. During the First World War the station handled some 35,000 animals (mainly horses and mules) arriving by train en route to the large re-mount depot at Shirehampton.

These increases in traffic because of the First World War led to further changes. On 2nd July 1917 platform tickets were introduced to capitalise on the large number of people using the station to see friends off and meeting others from overseas who had not transferred straight to through trains leaving the new Royal Edward Dock station. Facilities were also enhanced: the island platform was extended to 330 ft in December 1917 and a new cinder-covered up platform built and opened on 15th July 1918, the total cost of these two projects

being £7,420. Inter-platform connection was via an open footbridge adjacent to a level crossing at the west end of the station.

A small engine shed and a 60 ft turntable had come into use in January 1905 and December 1903 respectively. The engine shed closed in 1924 and the use of the turntable had ceased by the 1930s. A signal box at the far south-east end of the down platform was in use from 1903 to January 1969. Known as Avonmouth Dock Passenger signal box, it had 36 levers when it closed.

Despite the gradual improvements, the 1885 station, constructed largely of wood and corrugated iron, was by the mid-1920s proving completely inadequate for the number of passengers using the services. Thus, early in 1926, contractors began to rebuild the station. New brick buildings on the island platform included a large building with four

Station staff pose at the 1885 wooden station in about 1910 wearing Clifton Extension Railway (CER) uniforms. Left to right standing: Mr Percy Brunt, Mr Pickford, Mr Frederick Wheeler, Anon. Front sitting (left to right) Mr Reg Gore, Mr John Lait (station master), Mr Jones.

tall chimneys that incorporated most of the station facilities and a separate parcels office; work was completed by April of that year. The up platform (on the north side) which had been no more than a cinder track, was considerably improved and covered by a large wooden awning which is still in place today. Some commentators say that the major improvements were in part prompted by the imminent opening of the new Portway road from the centre of Bristol to Avonmouth along which operated a rival bus service. Staffing levels at Avonmouth Dock were for many years at a high level, for instance in 1913 there were 25 station staff and a further 47 handling goods traffic.

Avonmouth Dock station still operates today but the facilities are a pale reflection of their former glory. The old up platform (with the awning) serves trains while the main station building on the remaining wide island platform has gone. The site of the building, when viewed in March 2005, was occupied by cabins of Amey Engineering, working for Network Rail. The former brick parcels office near to Gloucester Road remains and is used as a hairdressing salon. The land originally in use for sidings on the bay side is now covered by industrial buildings. The wooden level crossing gates at the west end were replaced by full lifting barriers in September 1973. Although still in use for passengers, the station was closed to goods traffic on 20th June 1966.

Looking south east from the footbridge at the 1926 rebuilt station on 23rd August 1958. Off the picture to the right of the main building is the terminal bay.

Avonmouth Docks (Great Western)

OPENED: 9th May 1910 (as the terminus for trains running on the Filton – Henbury – Avonmouth line).

CLOSED: 22nd March 1915 (last train), 28th April 1919 (formal closure).

With the opening of the new line from Filton to Avonmouth via Henbury in May 1910, a new passenger service commenced linking the Avonmouth area with north Bristol. The rail motor trains were provided, for a short spell, with a terminus of their own some quarter of a mile south-west of the Avonmouth Dock station in Gloucester Road, almost adjacent to the Dock gates. It comprised a wooden platform with a wooden shelter. Along with the other stations on the line, it closed during the First World War as an economy measure in March 1915 but in this case did not re-open, though formal closure did not take place until April 1919. Today, some 90 years on, there are no remains to be seen of the station itself. However the site is clear on the right hand side of the road leading to the original main Dock entrance. It is behind two tall brick pillars close to the now locked gates, the remains of a pedestrian bridge over former dock lines that crossed Gloucester Road.

The only known photograph of this small station that operated as the terminus for local rail motor services on the Filton to Avonmouth line via Henbury. The station was only open from 1910 to 1915.

Avonmouth (Royal Edward Station)

OPENED: 20th April 1910 (first public use), 29th April 1910 (formal opening) (as the terminal station for boat trains to the new Royal Edward Dock).

CLOSED: 1941 (destroyed by enemy action). Boat trains subsequently used 'S' shed in a limited way until 26th August 1964.

From about 1900 a platform for rail passengers, with a baggage and waiting room, was in use at the landward end of the East Pier of Avonmouth Docks. However, with the opening of the new Royal Edward Dock on 9th July 1908, these facilities were clearly inadequate and a purpose built passenger station was constructed by the Port of Bristol on the South Pier.

The first passengers to actually use the new timber built station were from the ship *Port Kingston* on 20th April 1910. Reports at that time stated that the ship discharged 150 passengers and a 'mountain of luggage'. The formal opening ceremony, nine days later, was conducted by the Lord Mayor of Bristol, Alderman C.A. Hayes. During its construction the Bristol Docks Committee was accused of 'grave extravagance' and the projected new station was called the 'whitest of white elephants'! It was hoped, nevertheless, that the new passenger station would assist in making Avonmouth one of the most important passenger ports in the country and it did for some years with Avonmouth playing a particularly important role in emigration movements to the New World. In 1912 records indicate that 26,376 passengers travelled by rail to Avonmouth for embarkation. Regular trains ran via the new Henbury and Badminton cut-off routes to Paddington, taking between 2 and 2½ hours. Trains from the station were hauled first by special docks locomotives to a point near the Avonmouth Docks (GW) station where GWR locomotives were attached to the other end to haul the long trains north along the estuary to the Henbury line at Holesmouth Junction. Virtually all boat specials used this route.

The station was well equipped for all this traffic with a booking office (staffed by both the GWR and Midland Railway), waiting rooms, buffet, parcels office, telegraph office, baggage room and customs room. The original platform was some 500 ft long and this was lengthened in May 1911.

During the First World War a Mechanical Transport depot was established at Avonmouth Docks and for 2½ years the Dock was the embarkation point for motor vehicles. The new Dock station was taken over for use by this Depot.

The Royal Edward Dock station continued in major use during the inter-war period but was badly damaged and closed early in the Second World War. After the war the Port of Bristol Authority planned to rebuild it but plans were never fulfilled as passenger movements from Avonmouth Docks never regained the pre-war level. From 1941 S transit shed was used for the more limited passenger traffic with facilities for medical inspection and baggage examination. Until 1964 occasional passenger boat trains ran to the Docks; however, the last came to Avonmouth carrying passengers for the SS *Camito*, sailing to Trinidad, on 26th August 1964.

A general view from the south east of the 1910 station. Passenger trains entered and departed through the archway seen at the left of the building and passengers transferred to and from ships moored to the right. Customs and other facilities were in the central section.

A Port of Bristol Authority Peckett locomotive 0-6-0 ST pulls a train out of the station in September 1927. The ship is thought to be one of the Elders and Fyffes' fleet long associated with Avonmouth, in particular with the banana trade.

Crowds are gathered for the opening ceremony by the Lord Mayor of Bristol, Alderman C A Hayes on 29th April 1910.

Passengers inside the station in 1923. Note there were separate ticket windows operated by the Great Western and Midland Railways.

Bedminster

First Station

OPENED: June 1871 (on the Bristol Temple
          Meads – Weston-super-Mare
          – Taunton line originally opened
          through this site in 1841).
CLOSED: 27th May 1884.

Second Station

OPENED: 27th May 1884.
CLOSED: Passengers – remains open for local
          services on the Bristol Temple Meads
          – Weston-super-Mare – Taunton line.
          Goods – 1st June 1964.

Bedminster station, on the present site close to Fraser Street, opened on the then two track line to the south west in May 1884. An earlier 1871 station, some 250 yards to the east, closed at the same time. This 1871 station was sited at, or close to, an even earlier excursion platform which closed in about 1870. Extensions to the 1884 station, which included particularly attractive buildings with a number of ornate features and a footbridge at the west end, took place in 1908. Two photographs illustrate this second station prior to the early 1930s when complete re-building took place associated with quadrupling of the tracks.

The re-built station, opened on 30th April 1932, had more austere buildings on two island platforms between the four tracks; facilities included two waiting rooms, ticket and parcel offices and also a small siding to serve local coal merchants. Access to the platforms was via a long subway from the main station entrance on Fraser Street. Fifteen men were employed at Bedminster in 1938. Beyond the east end of the up platform stood a 74 lever signal box in use from April 1932 until April 1970.

Throughout its life Bedminster has been used primarily by passengers on local trains to and from Temple Meads and other Bristol suburban stations. It was often a departure point for excursions to such resorts as Weston-super-Mare, Clevedon, Weymouth, Paignton and Torquay. It was also the destination for workers travelling to the nearby factories in Bedminster and occasionally acted as an interchange point for passengers wishing to travel on the Portishead line.

A book by D.J. Fleming *Raising the Echos* (1984) describes well the lively scene at Bedminster station in the early 1950s: 'Bedminster was our local station, its platforms were swept daily, during the summer months the flower beds were ablaze with colour. Bees winged their way happily amongst the variety of blooms whose scent filled the air. During the colder months a roaring fire in the waiting room welcomed travellers. Great pride was taken in the station's appearance.'

Some 30 years later in 1979 Mr Fleming returned to Bedminster station and described what he called 'a scene full of sadness'. 'The station buildings have long since vanished. Today very few people echo through its once busy subways. Gone are the flower beds – the trolleys which once rumbled along the platforms.'

The station today is little different from that in 1979 with only local trains on the Weston-super-Mare and Taunton line calling at the island platforms. Goods services were withdrawn from Bedminster in June 1964; staffing ceased in September 1968. When visited in March 2005 a recent glass and metal shelter stood on each of the two island platforms; also provided were two small backless metal seats. The east ends of the two platforms were barred to public access. The subway walls were decorated with a coloured mural illustrating Bristol scenes including a train on the Portishead line passing under the Clifton Suspension Bridge and also a view of the SS *Great Britain*. The outer up track through the station was clearly in regular use but the down relief showed little sign of recent use.

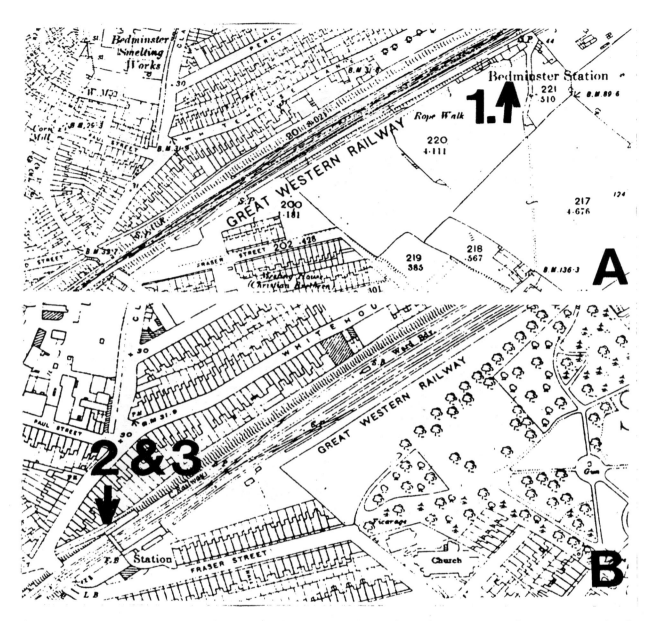

Bedminster Stations. Map A, an extract from an OS 1884 six inch edition, shows the station on its first site. Map B, dated 1903, shows the site on Fraser Street of Bedminster's second and third stations.

Looking north east at the 1884 station on the then two track line. A train to the west country passes under the impressive footbridge.

The fine entrance of the 1884 station facing on to Fraser Street. A train stands under the footbridge (left).

Locomotive 5565 passes through the rebuilt station with two island platforms en route to Portishead on 15th July 1956.

THEN A general view north east of Bedminster in 1964. To the left in the distance are early multi-storey blocks in central Bristol and to the right trees in Victoria Park.

NOW In about the same position 41 years later on 19th March 2005. The ex-Glasgow via Bristol (1510) Virgin Voyager passes through en route to Penzance. A modern metal and glass shelter serves passengers on the down island platform. Long sections of the former island platforms where the buildings stood are fenced off in the distance.

Brislington

OPENED: 3rd September 1873 (with the opening of the Bristol – Radstock line).

CLOSED: Passengers – 2nd November 1959.
Goods – 7th October 1963.

Brislington station opened in September 1873 on the single track Bristol and North Somerset Railway to Radstock. The facilities, of a standard B&NSR design, primarily comprised a brick building with three tall chimneys and a wooden horizontal fretted canopy on a platform some 365 ft long. This was situated on the down (east) side of the line, accessed by Station Road leading from Talbot Road to the north. Attractive gardens were a feature for many years as at many of the B&NSR stations. A platform extension was added at the northern end in 1908. A small signal box originally stood at the southern end of the platform controlling six signals and two sets of points; by 1908 the box had been replaced by a ground frame at the southern end of the station site. In the same year another ground frame came into use at the northern end.

Brislington goods yard was opposite the station building and platform on the up side of the line. Until 1908 there was only one siding; two new sidings were then laid connecting to the through line north of the station close to the Talbot Road overbridge. A new approach road to the goods yard from the west side of this bridge was also constructed in that year.

The function of the station was primarily for passengers travelling to and from Temple Meads station. In 1903 8,316 passenger tickets were issued; this rose slightly to 8,509 in 1913. Workers at the nearby Robertson's factory, opened in 1915, also used the station for travelling to and from work. It is believed, however, that freight from Robertson's

Looking north at the attractive station in about 1930. A member of the station staff is tending the garden, an outstanding feature at Brislington. Talbot Road bridge crosses the single track line in the distance.

THEN A general view south from Talbot Road bridge. Robertson's jam factory dominates the scene behind the station. The two goods sidings are empty.

NOW A desolate scene looking south from Talbot Road bridge on 21st March 2005. In the foreground is a section of a car park developed in the former railway cutting and under the bridge. The edge of the former platform can be seen (centre left) while a supermarket has replaced the Robertson's factory.

The beautiful garden south of the platform in about 1900. The station master stands in this fine example of a station garden with the name picked out in whitened stones, a common feature of many stations at that time.

was never despatched from Brislington but was sent by road to Temple Meads. Excursion trains also ran on occasions down the line to Radstock en route to the south and south west coast resorts, picking up at Brislington station. In March 1925 the staff comprised a station master and two porters.

Passenger services were withdrawn in November 1959 and the goods yard closed in October 1963. Much scrap material and coal was handled in the yard in the 1950s and 1960s and these merchants continued to use the yard after the rail facilities ceased. The line through Brislington closed completely on 10th July 1968.

For some years remains of the main building and platform stood at the side of the scrapyard and could be seen from the back of the Tesco store, built on the site of Robertson's factory and a section of the railway. These remains could also be seen from the Talbot Road bridge to the north. The station building has now gone but remnants of the platform can still be glimpsed in an otherwise derelict site. A small section of old railway fencing is still in place at the west end of the Talbot Road bridge adjacent to the former goods yard entrance. The old Station Road access to the east of the bridge is now sealed off by a tall steel fence; metal posts that originally carried the road name board remain behind the fence.

Chittening Platform

OPENED: 13th November 1918 (on the Filton – Henbury – Avonmouth line originally opened through this site in 1910; replaced the earlier Chittening Factory Platform on the Avonmouth – Pilning line).

CLOSED: 11th October 1923.

RE-OPENED: 31st May 1948 (to general public).

CLOSED: 23rd November 1964.

Also unadvertised opening for workmen 27th October 1941 – 1st August 1946 and 25th August 1947 – 30th May 1948.

During the First World War a number of railway developments took place in the Avonmouth area associated with the proposed establishment of a large government factory. In 1915 a workmen's platform called Chittening Factory was opened on the 1900 Avonmouth – Pilning freight line. New sidings were laid linked to the Filton to Avonmouth line (via Henbury) which had been completed in 1910. Chittening Platform opened on this latter line in November 1918 and closed some five years later in October 1923. This replaced the 1915 Chittening Factory Platform. The Second World War saw the unadvertised opening of a platform on the earlier 1918 site on 27th October 1941. It closed again on 1st August 1946 but re-opened for workmen on 25th August 1947. The official public opening of the basic platform and corrugated shelters, linked by an open metal footbridge at the east end, took place on 31st May 1948. Having served local factories for 16 years, it closed for good on 23rd November 1964 and no traces can now be found. For some years a parallel row of old concrete posts running south from the A403 road, south of the Chittening Estate, to the railway embankment marked the position of the old pedestrian approach to the platform but this has now gone covered by modern development, the Severn Park Fire and Rescue Training Centre.

Looking east in 1964. Two basic shelters and an open footbridge serve passengers at the exposed location.

Clifton Bridge

OPENED: 18th April 1867 (with the opening of the Portishead branch).

CLOSED: Passengers – 7th September 1964.
Goods – 5th July 1965.

Clifton Bridge station opened in April 1867 on the new broad gauge Bristol to Portishead line. To avoid confusion with Clifton Down station which opened in 1874, and also with the originally named Clifton terminus of the Hotwells to Avonmouth line opened in 1865, Clifton Bridge station was re-named Rownham in March 1891. The name reverted to Clifton Bridge in 1910.

The main station facilities on the down (west) side comprised a long building facing the road entrance on the A369. Within this building one long room ran the length of the ground floor, which was partitioned into a waiting room (entrance direct from the platform), a booking office and a station master's office. In addition there was a coal-fired boiler room providing hot water for washing facilities. Entering the building from the large station forecourt, passengers turned right into the booking office. Upstairs there was spacious living accommodation accessed by a private staircase. For some years from the early days the station had an excellent garden alongside this down platform.

The early 1880s saw a number of developments at the station brought about by track changes.

Between 24th and 27th January 1880 the line was converted from broad to standard gauge. Later that year, on 15th September, a crossing loop was brought into use at the station and a second up platform with a substantial shelter was added on the river side. The two platforms were partly covered by canopies described as 'half barrel' or 'umbrella' type. A footbridge at the south end of the station provided a link between the platforms; it also carried a public footpath. The crossing loop was incorporated into the complete doubling of the line between Portishead Junction to just north of Clifton Bridge station on 2nd September 1883. A small signal cabin on the up platform immediately south of the shelter was closed on 25th August 1907. It was replaced by a larger box off the southern end of the up platform; with 27 levers it closed on 4th November 1966. It is recorded that Clifton Bridge station was flooded to a depth of several feet in 1899 when severe flooding affected several parts of Bristol including areas of Bedminster and Ashton.

Clifton Bridge station was set in an open area at the southern end of the main Avon Gorge, the scene being dominated by the Suspension Bridge from which the station derived its name. The *Bristol Times and Mirror* of 20th April 1867 (two days after the station opened) referred to 'a bustling railway station under the shadow of Rownham Hill'. In the early days the station was served by horse buses,

Looking north towards the Clifton Suspension Bridge. A down rail motor with trailer en route to Portishead is at the down platform in about 1906. The first small signal cabin stands on the up platform adjacent to the shelter, the back wall of which remains in place today.

A rare view south in 1963 showing the short bay goods platform (right) linked to the down line.

Clifton Bridge, (Bristol) 1954

CB Swallow 021

The principal building facing west towards the A369 Portishead road in 1954. The site is now redeveloped for the Avon and Somerset Police Horse and Dog Section.

THEN Looking north from the footbridge in 1963. The second August 1907 signal box which replaced the platform cabin is glimpsed at the bottom right. Note the station garden including a greenhouse behind the down platform.

NOW Looking north from the recently re-vamped footbridge on 21st April 2005. Remains of the down platform are still in place (left) alongside the re-laid single line carrying freight trains to Royal Portbury Dock. The Avon and Somerset Police building is behind the tall trees (top left).

running from Tyndall's Park Road through Clifton over the Suspension Bridge and down Rownham Hill. Passengers could also reach the station by catching the horse bus at the Corn Exchange in the city centre; this brought them to the Rownham Ferry at Hotwells which provided the final link across the river to the station.

For many years, until its demise in 1932, the Rownham Ferry provided a key link to Clifton Bridge station. The ferry took dock and power station workers living in the Hotwells and Clifton areas across the river to catch trains to Portishead; in addition it was useful for members of the public who wished to take a train trip through the attractive gorge. In the reverse direction the station was also used by commuters from Portishead who either caught the ferry or walked across the Cumberland Basin bridges to work in the city docks or Hotwells areas. The latter was only possible after the opening of the new Ashton Swing Bridge over the New Cut in 1906. Finally the station was good for walkers from Bristol wishing to access the riverside path on the Somerset side of the Avon.

The year 1878 saw a royal occasion at Clifton Bridge station when the then Prince of Wales visited the Royal Agricultural Society's Show being held on the Downs. The Prince arrived in the city at Temple Meads station by a special train from London; he travelled through the city in a horse and carriage and, having visited the Show, was driven across the Downs and over the Suspension Bridge to Clifton Bridge station where the special train was waiting to take him to his next destination.

The outbreak of the First World War led to great increases in the volume of freight traffic on the railways; at one point a 50% increase in passenger fares was introduced to curb passenger traffic and most excursion trains to resorts and special events ceased running. This immediately affected Clifton Bridge station as it had started to play a major role in bringing passengers to the Bristol International Exhibition known as the 'White City' which opened on Ashton Meadows on 29th June 1914. The Exhibition came to an early end on 15th August 1914 when it was taken over by the War Office as barracks for army recruits.

A further impact of the First World War was the establishment at Clifton Bridge station of a special mule depot (a foretaste of today's role of the site as the headquarters of the Avon and Somerset Mounted Police?). The depot handled mule traffic from all the local docks before the animals were transported by train to military camps, for instance locally to Shirehampton or to Salisbury Plain. As a wartime expedient Clifton Bridge station closed to passengers on Sundays for a period from January 1917. During the 1930s there was an average of eight staff based at the station.

The Second World War saw intensive passenger activity along the Portishead line with many Bristol residents evacuated to the Pill and Portbury areas. A large number of these evacuees travelled into work on the early trains, a number getting off at Clifton Bridge station to walk into Ashton or over the Cumberland Basin bridges. During the air raids people slept in the nearby Clifton Bridge No 1 Tunnel or in railway carriages stored in the station sidings. Between 1942 and 1944 the station master was James Henry Almond, whilst the staff included two ladies, a Mrs Durbin and a Miss Lancastle, working full time as porters. Also during the war period members of the Women's Land Army loaded timber from nearby woods onto trains at the station. A short goods siding linked to the down line served a bay goods platform at the north end of the down platform. Freight traffic generated by the Ashton Containers factory was handled at the station; all labelling was undertaken there but accountancy was handled at Temple Meads. Records indicate that a local firm based in Leigh Woods with a trade in herbal medicine also used Clifton Bridge, the trucks mainly going to South Wales.

After the war traffic levels declined and the station was downgraded to a halt and unstaffed as from 29th October 1962. Eventually the station was closed to passengers, along with the rest of the Portishead branch, on 7th September 1964. Closure to goods traffic came less than a year later on 5th July 1965. The track through Clifton Bridge station had been singled in May of that year but the branch remained open for freight traffic until 1981.

Today the site of the main station building is covered by the buildings of the headquarters of the Avon and Somerset Constabulary Mounted Police and Dog Section. The edge of the former down platform, a section of the rear wall of the up side shelter and the recently re-vamped footbridge are, however, still in place alongside the open space parallel to the river and Route 41 of the National Cycle Network. The track through the station has been re-laid to accommodate freight trains serving Royal Portbury Dock. The formal re-opening of the line took place on 21st December 2001 and the first commercial working operated on 7th January 2002.

Clifton Down

OPENED: 1st October 1874 (as the initial terminus of the Clifton Extension Railway).

CLOSED: Passengers – remains open for services on the Bristol Temple Meads – Avonmouth – Severn Beach line.
Goods – 5th July 1965.

Clifton Down station opened in October 1874 as the temporary terminus of the Clifton Extension Railway that ran west from the Bristol to South Wales line at Narroways Hill Junction and the Midland Railway at Kingswood Junction. It became a through station for passengers on 1st September 1885 when passenger services commenced through the Clifton Down Tunnel, linking with the 1865 Hotwells to Avonmouth line. However, a number of services continued to terminate at Clifton Down. Goods traffic through the tunnel had commenced eight years earlier on 24th February 1877.

Commentators describe Clifton Down station in its heyday as 'commodious and handsome' and indeed it was. The buildings, in a 'modified Gothic' style cost some £20,000; the principal building on the up (north) side incorporated a lofty and spacious booking hall with a huge fireplace at each end. Constructed of squared random stone with a two-storey centrepiece, it was of a typical mid-Victorian design. Pointed ground floor doorways led into the spacious hall on each side of which were the usual offices and waiting rooms. This large two-storey up side building is believed to have been constructed to house the station master, a common practice in the nineteenth century, but it is thought it was never used for this. Leading down to these buildings from Whiteladies Road was a wide carriage drive at the entrance to which, on the northern side, was the Imperial Hotel (now Canynge Hall, part of Bristol University). At the head of the drive a cabman's rest was erected at a cost of £75; each cabman paid 4d a week for its use.

A further outstanding feature of Clifton Down station was the extensive platforms; sited on a slight curve the down platform was 481 ft long and 2 ft 11½ inches high and the up platform 500 ft long and 3 ft 2½ inches high. Each platform was originally covered for much of its length by a 'ridge and furrow' fluted glass roof supported by a series of iron columns. In the 1930s these canopies were partially removed; damage occurred during the Second World War and total removal came in May 1971. There was originally no waiting room on the down platform; however, one was provided in October 1898 at a cost of £300. In 1887 the Automatic Weighing Company placed two machines at the station for an annual sum of £15 each. The two platforms were linked by a glass-covered bridge, approached on each side through impressive arches. Clifton Down station together with Montpelier station, was built by Messrs Baker & Son of Canons Marsh, Bristol, whilst records show that the platforms were covered with asphalt supplied by Mr Bradshaw of Totterdown. In August 1883 the station was flooded and extra drains were installed to prevent a recurrence.

With the growing number of potential passengers in the developing suburbs of north and west Bristol, both the Great Western and Midland Railways who jointly built the Clifton Extension Railway, were anxious to link the trains on this line to other principal services into and out of Bristol. Links with the Great Western trains were made generally at Temple Meads or Stapleton Road, whilst links to the Midland Railway trains, running to and from the north and Bath, were made at Fishponds or Mangotsfield. Most of the Clifton Extension Railway trains left Temple Meads shortly after the arrival of principal trains from London. Even at the start of services at Clifton Down station in 1874 (before the Clifton Down Tunnel opened) there were 46 arrivals and departures a day, 23 trains each way. A Midland service to St Philips station also commenced with the through service from Avonmouth on 1st September 1885; this service ceased, however, after only a month. In February 1876 a new service between Weston-super-Mare and Clifton Down started and on 1st September 1885 was extended through the Clifton Down Tunnel to Avonmouth.

In April 1910 17 down and 15 up trains between Bristol and Avonmouth stopped at Clifton Down, whilst 20 Great Western Railway trains terminated at Clifton Down. In addition the Midland Railway ran 13 trains each way between Mangotsfield or Fishponds and Clifton Down. These Midland trains ceased on 1st January 1917 but were restored on 5th May 1919. Permanent withdrawal of these Midland Railway services came on 31st March 1941, as a wartime measure.

Throughout its history Clifton Down station has been an important facility for either the departure

THEN On 1st May 1907 a number of Prime Ministers from the then British Empire travelled from the station to Avonmouth to view construction work at the new Royal Edward Dock. Carriages are seen arriving for the 2.50 pm departure.

NOW The entrance arch to the up platform some 98 years later on 31st March 2005. Extensive refurbishment of the archways and reinstatement of the footbridge between them was a feature of work undertaken in 1992/93. Note that the lamp on the archway is higher than in 1907, apparently considered more vandal proof! Top right the car park of the Clifton Down shopping centre dominates.

or arrival of excursion trains. Excursions from Clifton Down, in common with many other stations in Bristol, ran to Weston-super-Mare, Clevedon, and to the south coast and south west resorts. Regular daily excursion trains from Clifton Down to Clevedon and Weston-super-Mare began on 8th July 1921 and continued throughout the summer season. Records show that 10 years earlier, in 1911, a new feature was the excursion trains to and from London running chiefly on Wednesdays and Saturdays. These often started at about 4 a.m. and returned about 24 hours later. Connecting trains to Stapleton Road often ran from Clifton Down so that excursionists could catch special trains to the north. Special services ran from Clifton Down station and other suburban stations to Ashton Gate for football matches. Summer Bank Holidays often saw the suspension of normal services in favour of through trains to Weston-super-Mare. On 28th June 1925 the station saw its first Sunday half day excursion to Weymouth leaving at 11.20 a.m. with arrival in Weymouth at 2.00 p.m. Two trains ran, 2,260 passengers were carried and the fare was five shillings.

Equally important for Clifton Down station was the arrival of special excursion traffic. In 1886 Clifton Down station dealt with an enormous influx associated with the Bath and West show held on Durdham Down on the 2nd, 3rd, 4th, 5th, and 7th June. The total Show attendance over the five days was some 100,532; the number dealt with at Clifton Down station during this period being 33,733. On each of the five days three special fast trains ran from Bath to Clifton Down and back. On the Saturday of the Show normal services were suspended with trains to and from Temple Meads every 20 minutes. On Saturday 5th June 47 trains ran from Temple Meads instead of the normal 31. During the Show extra station staff were brought in. In 1921 the Bath and West Show was again held on the Downs with a total attendance of over 100,000 and again 12 special trains ran to and from Clifton Down station. Demand, however, seems to have been less than on the earlier occasion because of road competition which included a bus service direct from Temple Meads station to the Downs.

Excursions to Clifton Down station for Bristol Zoo, known as 'Monkey Specials', were a feature for many years, especially from South Wales. They ran mid-week every Tuesday, Wednesday and Thursday from the end of May to the end of August. These continued into the early 1970s and indeed between 1958 and 1966 some 340,000 such excursion passengers were dealt with at the station. Sometimes as many as three or four trains came on one day. The closure of many of the Welsh Valley lines and the opening of the Severn Road Bridge in 1966 led to the demise of the 'Monkey Specials'. Until the early 1960s Clifton Down station also dealt with circus traffic when such shows were held on the Downs.

Royal visits have also featured at Clifton Down station, for instance in 1902 and 1908. On Wednesday 5th March 1902 the Prince of Wales turned the first sod of the new Royal Edward Dock at Avonmouth. Having spent the previous night at Badminton House, the royal train arrived at Temple Meads at 12.10 p.m. where the royal party got out on Platform 5. The train left for Clifton Down where it arrived at about 12.30 p.m. and was shunted into the up platform with the royal saloon opposite the Midland entrance door to the booking office. Their Royal Highnesses joined the train again at Clifton Down after they had driven through the city from Temple Meads; the special train departed at 12.45 p.m. A similar procedure took place on 9th July 1908 when the now King Edward VII returned to open the Royal Edward Dock. On this occasion the King and Queen actually travelled to Bristol by the London and North Western royal train on 8th July and stayed on the Royal Yacht at Avonmouth. On 9th July, following transport from Avonmouth by the GWR royal train, they drove through the city from Temple Meads to Clifton Down embarking on the royal train at about 3.00 p.m., Avonmouth being reached at 3.20 p.m. The opening ceremony of the new Dock followed. Apart from the time the line was closed for the royal train, the Clifton Extension Railway was very busy on that day taking passengers to and from the opening ceremony at Avonmouth. Fame had also come to Clifton Down station with the arrival in 1907 of a number of Prime Ministers from the Empire, also on a visit to Avonmouth.

Throughout its history Clifton Down station also handled a considerable volume of goods traffic. Coal was the principal commodity with at times 30–40 wagons a day being dealt with in the extensive goods yard, with a crane of 5 ton capacity, to the south of the station buildings. At busy times some passenger trains were stored in this yard. Parcel traffic was also considerable. Strange as it may seem, for a period during the 1880s Clifton Down station was a forwarding point for milk. In 1886 it is recorded that 151 cans of milk (1,491 gallons) were forwarded from the station for a total charge of £4.19s.3d. In 1887 none was handled, but in

THEN An excellent overall view, dated 31st May 1959, looking east showing the station and extensive goods yard. Buildings on Whiteladies Road are seen beyond.

NOW Again looking east from the same point on St Johns Road bridge. Taken on 7th June 2005 the large Clifton Down shopping centre and car park together with housing development cover the former goods yard. The principal station building remains in use as the 'Roo Bar' (left).

1889 21 cans (179 gallons) were handled at a cost of 16s.4d.

Clifton Down employed an average of 22 staff from 1903 until the 1930s. In 1958 there was still a station master, a chief booking clerk, two adult clerks, two lad clerks working in the booking office, six porters, a shunter, a checker and a weighbridge assistant. However, the goods yard closed in July 1965 and the station became unstaffed on 17th July 1967. A signal box stood at the west end of the down platform; with a 28-lever frame it remained in use until 18th November 1970 when the line from Ashley Hill to Avonmouth was generally singled, though a double track loop was retained through Clifton Down and remains today.

Clifton Down station today offers some evidence of its past glories. The main station building remains; over the years it has hosted a number of drinking and catering premises, in spring 2005, the Roo Bar. The back walls of the spacious platforms remain. For some years only the up side archway entrance remained in use, the down side arch bricked up. Access to the down platform was only via a concrete staircase at the east end of the platform from pavement level on Whiteladies Road. The covered passenger footbridge had been demolished. In 1992/1993 a programme of refurbishment was undertaken including the installation of a new open metal footbridge, the restoration of the two archways and the introduction of a long ramp to the down platform. Access to the up platform is either via steps beyond the archway at the east end of the platform or on the level at the west end from the station forecourt and access road. Shelter is provided today in two modern glass and metal structures, one on each platform.

Today, on a weekday, some 10 trains a day on the Severn Beach line call at Clifton Down each way, providing a well-used service for commuters and shoppers in north Bristol. Over the platform at the eastern end is a concrete 'raft' on which an undistinguished row of shops was built in the 1960s. Major development has been undertaken south of the station with the Clifton Down shopping centre and housing developments now covering virtually all the original goods yard.

A 1964 photograph looking east from the up platform. The detail of the roof and columns is very striking. Much of the roof over the down platform (right) had been removed both during the 1930s and following damage during the Second World War.

A further view this time looking west under the remaining section of the up platform roof. The signal box at the west end of the down platform controlled movements into and out of the extensive goods yard, the tracks to which are seen beyond the box adjacent to the tunnel entrance.

Fishponds

OPENED: 1st April 1866 (on the Bristol
– Gloucester line originally opened
through this site in 1844).

CLOSED: Passengers – 7th March 1966.
Goods – 13th December 1965.

Fishponds station opened in April 1866 on the Bristol to Gloucester line, which had originally opened to traffic some 22 years earlier on 8th July 1844. At its opening the station was named Stapleton; this changed to Fish Ponds in January 1867 and to Fishponds on 1st May 1939.

At its opening Fishponds station made its mark on railway history because of a dispute between the Board of Trade and the Midland Railway. The Board's inspecting officer, Captain Tyler, insisted that the new station was inspected to ensure that all arrangements had been made to ensure the safety of passengers even though the line itself had been open for many years. Until then new stations on existing lines had not been inspected.

A substantial brick and stone building with a large ridge and furrow glass canopy and ornamental chimneys stood on the up platform (towards Gloucester). The Midland (and later the LMS) Bristol District Control Office was housed in this up side building. A footbridge led to the down main platform and the bay platform. A link span connected the east side of the footbridge to the road bridge which crossed the line just north of the station. A brick shelter with chimneys and a horizontal fretted canopy served passengers on the down platform. The opportunity was taken to widen the platforms at Fishponds with the elimination of the broad gauge in 1872. Clifton Down and Avonmouth trains commenced and terminated at the bay platform from 1st October 1874 until 31st March 1941 (wartime closure 1st January 1917 – 15th May 1919).

At the southern end of the station, on the up side, Fishponds goods yard, with goods shed and a 5 ton crane primarily dealt with coal and china clay traffic for various local factories and merchants. A weighbridge building was located at the yard's road entrance. The yard had an access from Hockeys Lane/Lower Station Road. On the up side, north of the station and road bridge, a further set of sidings provided additional freight capacity; the first siding was laid in 1905; there were five when they ceased

Looking north east in 1959. Carriages stand at the up platform with the principal building behind. A shelter with canopy stands on the down island platform (right).

to be used in 1965. Finally, a siding from the down line, south of the station, ran into the adjacent Avonside Locomotive Works until these closed in 1935. Fishponds signal box, built in 1896 and with a new frame from 1905, was beyond the south-west end of the down platform. With 25 levers, it remained in use until 12th May 1968.

Fishponds station served three main passenger roles; firstly as a facility used by local residents travelling into Bristol or to the midlands and Gloucester, secondly, as a destination point for workers coming to the diverse local industries and thirdly, to a lesser degree, as a changing point for passengers travelling on the Clifton Down and Avonmouth line and transferring to the through trains to the north and to Bath via Mangotsfield. However, Fishponds' interchange role was less than

Like many Bristol stations Fishponds was the departure point for excursions. Here a large crowd is waiting on the down platform to board a number of trains departing for Weston-super-Mare on 23rd July 1907. The train at the platform appears to be full already! Note the many other carriages in the bay platform (top left).

that of Mangotsfield, further up the line towards Gloucester and Bath.

Terry Osborne, in his book *Memories of the Mangotsfield to Bath Branch and the local Railway Scene*, describes the scene in 1920: 'Fishponds was a very busy station. In all there would be about 72 passenger trains passing or stopping at Fishponds in 24 hours. The majority ran from 5.45 a.m. to 11.00 p.m. There were also all the goods and parcel trains. A lot of shunting also went on in the siding ... 29 stopping local trains from Fishponds to Bristol and Clifton Down. There were 30 local trains from Bristol to Gloucester and Bath stopping at Fishponds. Of these five each way were to and from Clifton Down with two of these starting at Fishponds station and the other three starting at Mangotsfield station.' In contrast in 1964-65 Osborne notes: 'The stopping trains at Fishponds to Bath and Gloucester main line were 12 and 13 from Bath and Gloucester to Bristol Temple Meads ... the track from Clifton Down station lifted.'

The last reference is to the Ashley Hill to Kingswood Junction line including the major viaduct at Eastville over the South Wales line which was closed to all traffic from 14th June 1965, the last passenger train to and from Clifton Down having run 24 years earlier on the 31st March 1941.

Fishponds station closed to goods traffic in December 1965 and to passengers in March 1966, the latter when passenger traffic on the Bath branch was withdrawn. The line through the station closed officially on 3rd January 1970. The last Bristol to Gloucester fast train passed through on 26th December 1969, the day before a landslide blocked the route.

Today the former station site is transformed. A section of the Bristol to Bath Cycleway passes through south-west to north-east, a part of the first long cycleway in the country that follows in general the trackbed of the former Bristol to Mangotsfield section of the line to Gloucester and the Mangotsfield to Bath branch. For some years the cycleway ran along the former Fishponds down platform which survived along with the up platform long after the station buildings were demolished. In recent years the area has become dominated by a supermarket and its associated new roads to the west of the former station site. Construction of the roads covered a section of the trackbed in and north of the station and also involved the demolition of the road over rail bridge. As a result the cycleway, for a short section, deviates slightly south-east from the original alignment of the trackbed and passes

THEN A general view south on 14th March 1932 taken from the station footbridge. The principal building with its impressive ridge and furrow canopy and tall chimneys is on the up platform (towards Gloucester). The bay platform used by trains to Clifton Down and Avonmouth is on the far left. The building seen at the extreme left is that of the Avonside Locomotive works.

NOW Over 70 years later on 29th April 2005 the scene has drastically changed when viewed from almost the identical point. Road works led to many changes including the removal of the original road bridge north of the station. The inverted fish sculpture stands approximately on the site of the former down platform. The distant industrial building (former George Adlam) is the only remaining feature from the 1932 photo.

through a new road bridge that carries the west end of Filwood Road. A tall brick structure in the shape of a fish constructed by Wimpy apprentices stands beside the cycleway approximately on the site of the former down platform. The old goods yard is now the southern section of the supermarket car park. The former sidings north-west of the station are now covered by modern industrial buildings accessed off a new road, New Station Way. For many years this area had been occupied by a local coal merchant.

The station master (front row centre) with his staff in about 1922 on the up platform close to the footbridge. Hoardings include adverts for Cerebos salt, Puritan soap and Foster Clark's custard.

Henbury

OPENED: 9th May 1910 (with the opening of the Filton – Avonmouth line).

CLOSED: Passengers – 23rd November 1964.
Goods – 5th July 1965.
Temporary closure for advertised passenger services 22nd March 1915 – 10th July 1922.

Henbury station opened in May 1910 on the new single track direct line from Filton to Avonmouth. In addition to the accommodation for passengers, facilities were provided for goods traffic including agricultural produce in a small goods yard with cattle pens to the south-east of the station. The principal red brick building and original platform were sited on the south side of the line. The building incorporated from west to east the station master's office, the booking office and general waiting room, the ladies waiting room and a gent's urinal. An unusual feature was a goldfish pond on the platform. Immediately to the east of the building was a small red brick office.

During the First World War stations and halts on this line were closed as a wartime expedient and to release railway staff for other wartime duties and thus Henbury station closed to the public on 22nd March 1915. However it continued to be used by unadvertised workmen's services, a maximum of 6,600 workers using the station daily. It did not re-open to the public until 10th July 1922, although in 1917 the line was doubled, associated with wartime developments in the area. A second platform and shelter were added on the north side in advance of laying the second track. Inter-platform movements were via steps leading to the adjacent road bridge to the west. Three men were employed at the station in the 1920s and 1930s. During the First World War it had one claim to fame as on the night of 8th November 1917 the King and Queen were in residence in the royal train, stabled overnight at the station.

Passenger services to and from Henbury station included circular trips from Temple Meads to Avonmouth via this line and through Clifton Down. Passenger services ceased in November 1964 and the station closed to goods traffic in July 1965. The line through Henbury station was singled as from 22nd May 1966. Double track was re-introduced in summer 1992 to cater for the 'merry-go-round' coal trains from Avonmouth to the Didcot and Aberthaw power stations. Today sections of the south side platform remain but that on the north side has now gone, the final sections being demolished with the recent re-introduction of double track. The main brick building, the small brick office, and an adjacent weighbridge are still there. For some years the main building acted as an office for a coal merchant but in spring 2005 it was disused, as was the small former office. The station forecourt and the former goods yard are today occupied by a number of stone aggregates firms. Two former goods yard entrance gate posts are still in place behind the main building.

Looking west in 1955 at this attractive station on the northern edge of Bristol. Brick buildings with wooden canopies serve passengers on both platforms.

THEN Looking east from Station Road bridge in 1964. A small signal box stands beyond the far end of the north side platform.

NOW A view east, again from Station Road bridge, over 40 years later on 5th April 2005. The north side platform has gone but sections of the south platform remain. The principal station building still stands, currently disused, on the south side hidden by trees and bushes (centre).

Horfield

OPENED: 14th May 1927 (on the Bristol – South Wales line originally opened through this site in 1863).
CLOSED: Passengers – 23rd November 1964. Goods – facilities never provided.

Horfield opened in May 1927 as a small facility on the then double track line to South Wales. At its opening facilities were minimal with a wooden shelter on the two platforms, accessed by steps and paths from either side of the railway cutting. To the west there was housing development and to the east the access path led from open land later to be built upon in the Lockleaze development.

In the early 1930s the South Wales line was quadrupled through Horfield and thus a complete rebuild of the station was necessary in the cutting, widened on the east side when the two extra tracks were laid. The rebuilt facility comprised an island platform and two side platforms, each with a shelter. The original down (towards Filton) platform was retained and extended and the three platforms were linked by a long footbridge. No footbridge had been provided at the earlier 1927 station, access to the platform being via steps from the adjacent high road

bridge. Access to the whole station was now via a new long path from the Melton Crescent western end of the road bridge; there was now no direct access from the east side. At road level, a wooden building supported on wooden baulks incorporated a ticket office and toilet facilities.

Originally named Horfield Platform, the new station was opened and re-named Horfield on 30th April 1933. Closure to passengers came on 23rd November 1964. Goods facilities were never provided. One notable feature in its history came in November 1953 when the *Evening Post* recorded that 10 Bristol Rovers fans were 'locked in Horfield railway station for 10 hours after the game at Coventry'. Today the location of the entrance to the ticket office and access path from the road bridge can still be identified, the gap in the wall filled by a small section of open metal fence. An old piece of track acting as a post and a short section of former railway fencing are also still there next to the entrance. Sections of the two side platforms can also be seen at the base of the cutting, south of the road bridge. The number of tracks running south to north through the station site reduced from four to two in 1984.

Looking south in 1928 at the basic facilities of Horfield Platform as it was then known. Small shelters serve passengers on the platforms on the then two track line. Steps provide access from either side.

A view from the south east of the much expanded 1933 station on 18th August 1963. The access path and steps lead down from the precariously sited booking office at the west end of Bonnington Walk road bridge. Concrete shelters serve passengers on the two side and one island platform.

A close-up of the booking office entrance at the west end of the Bonnington Walk road bridge dated 18th September 1955.

THEN Looking south at Horfield from the high Bonnington Walk road bridge at the 1933 station. Note the clear evidence of the widening of the cutting on the east side to accommodate the expanded station and four tracks. Access is now only from the west side via the concrete steps and long footbridge. The Lockleaze housing area has not yet developed.

NOW From the same viewpoint on the road bridge on 14th March 2005. The 1506 Wessex Trains Class 158 from Weston-super-Mare to Great Malvern passes through the station site, the only remains being platform edges on either side of the deep cutting.

Hotwells

OPENED: 6th March 1865 (as the southern terminus of the Bristol Port Railway and Pier line).

CLOSED: Passengers – 19th September 1921.
Goods – 1st September 1890.

Hotwells station opened in March 1865 as the southern terminus of the Bristol Port Railway and Pier Company's line to Avonmouth. Situated in a rather cramped location in the Avon gorge almost beneath the Suspension Bridge (and just north of today's road canopy), the station was originally called Clifton but was re-named Hotwells in March 1891 to avoid confusion with Clifton Down and Clifton Bridge stations. (At the same time the latter was re-named Rownham, though later restored to Clifton Bridge.) Hotwells station originally had three lines: a platform line, a run-round loop and a carriage siding, all linked by a turntable. This turntable feature was not liked by the Board of Trade and was later removed, probably in 1893 when the main platform was lengthened to 280 ft. An early small locomotive shed was burnt down in 1873 and replaced two years later by a shed at Shirehampton.

A two-storey stone building was sited at the terminal end of the platform, the track being level with the upper storey. A booking office was located on the ground floor and passengers mounted a flight of steps to a landing which connected with a waiting room and, until 1893, a refreshment room. When the latter closed the space was converted to an additional waiting room and office accommodation. The water tank at the station was connected to the mains and locomotives filled up at every visit. The normal staffing at Hotwells was a station master and porter.

At its opening on 6th March 1865 it is said that the proposed timetable was purposely withheld from the public and only posted a few minutes before the departure of the first train for fear that the crowd would be such that the one locomotive could not cope. An over-crowded train would also not have created a good impression; it appears that the result was the railway operated one of the emptiest inaugural trains in history!

One of Hotwells station's busiest days was at the opening of the original Avonmouth Docks on 24th February 1877. The Company ran trains every half hour and there was a great crush with police having to control an estimated 20,000 passengers who used the line that day. Workers at Avonmouth Docks and trippers going to the leisure facilities at Avonmouth (for example the Avonmouth Hotel and pleasure grounds) were the principal regular users of Hotwells station. It is recorded that on 12th January 1899 a very high tide flooded the lower storey of the station and passengers were transported to and from the trains by boat.

A close-up of the station buildings enlarged from the 1910 photograph on page 77. The two-storey building with the booking office at ground level stands at the terminus of the three tracks on one of which carriages are stored. The wall has an advertisement for Harry Roy in 'Made in England' at the Empire Theatre in Bristol.

A view along the gorge from the lower station of the Clifton Rocks Railway which linked Hotwells to Clifton until its closure in 1934. Hotwells station can be seen in the distance beyond the tram which is running on the service between the station and Arnos Vale.

Railway staff pose at the terminus in the 1890s in front of an Avonmouth bound train hauled by a GWR 0-4-2T locomotive.

Clifton Rocks from Leigh Woods, Bristol. 651.

THEN A view across the Avon gorge from Leigh Woods in about 1910. The station nestles at the foot of the cliffs immediately below the observatory.

NOW The view some 95 years later on 8th May 2005 which pinpoints the former station site adjacent to the north end of the modern road canopy.

THEN Looking down from the east end of the Clifton Suspension Bridge in about 1913. Passengers are alighting from an Avonmouth train. People stroll beside the banks of the Avon (left), the Portway road came here some years later. Note the employees' vegetable plots at the foot of the cliff (right).

NOW Again looking down from the same point on the bridge on 8th May 2005. Trees and bushes cover the site of the station. The now sealed tunnel that carried the railway north under Bridge Valley Road is clear. Road traffic runs on the 80 year old Portway.

A horse-drawn tramway was opened in the 1880s, linking the station to the city centre (the Drawbridge). This proved a considerable boon to the railway. The tramway was electrified on 22nd December 1900.

The importance of Hotwells station declined from the time the Avonmouth line was linked to the main Bristol rail network in 1874 (goods) and in 1885 (passengers), via the Clifton Extension Railway at Sneyd Park Junction. Goods facilities at the station were withdrawn from 1st September 1890. Final closure at Hotwells station did not come, however, until 19th September 1921 when a section of the track bed in the gorge was required for the construction of the new Portway road to Avonmouth.

Hotwells Halt

OPENED: 14th May 1917 (on the Hotwells
               – Avonmouth line originally opened
               through this site in 1865).
CLOSED: 3rd July 1922.

Hotwells Halt opened in May 1917 as a wartime expedient for long workmen's trains that could not be accommodated at Hotwells station, whose cramped site prevented expansion. The wooden platform was some 700 ft long and could accommodate trains of up to eight bogie coaches that were needed at this time to transport the large number of workers to the Docks. It is said that in the morning up to 2,000 workmen used to travel by tram to the main Hotwells terminus station and then walk along the towpath past 'Point Villa' (at a location near Bridge Valley Road), kept by a Mrs George who sold refreshments. When the workmen arrived at the new timber platform they walked up a ramp to one of the two new ticket huts. The porter in the smaller hut only issued Avonmouth tickets whilst the station master in the larger hut had a greater range of tickets.

Situated at the north end of the platform was a signal box which controlled both the entrance to a line used for storing the long workmen's trains and a run-round loop. After the early morning rush hour the main Hotwells station was normally used. Congestion was not as great in the evenings as the workmen's ticket returns issued at Hotwells were valid for return to either Hotwells itself or Clifton Down station. Some workmen thus took advantage of this and returned to Clifton Down station and walked home thus saving the tram fare from Hotwells to the city centre.

For nearly 10 months Hotwells Halt acted as the final terminus of the Hotwells spur, as the track bed of that section of the line was not wanted initially for the Portway road. Formal closure of Hotwells Halt came, after its brief enhanced status, on 3rd July 1922, though the records indicate that it was last used on the 1st.

With no known photograph, the only record is that of a Samuel Loxton 1919 drawing of the 700 ft long wooden platform in use for five years from 1917 to 1922.

Lawrence Hill

OPENED: 8th September 1863 (with the opening of the Bristol and South Wales Union Railway Bristol Temple Meads – New Passage Pier).

CLOSED: Passengers – remains open for local services on the Bristol – Gloucester, Cardiff and Avonmouth/Severn Beach lines.
Goods – 29th November 1965.

Lawrence Hill station opened as a small facility with one platform on the west side of the single track Bristol and South Wales Union Railway in September 1863. The line through the station was doubled in 1874 and a second platform added. In November 1891 quadrupling of the line through Lawrence Hill was completed, the new tracks being laid on the east side of the two 1874 tracks. The station was rebuilt and much enlarged with substantial structures on an island and two outer platforms. A particular feature was the large covered footbridge linking the platforms over the four tracks. These structures remained in place for some 80 years but were largely demolished in August 1970; the footbridge had been removed earlier, inter-platform pedestrian links being via the road bridge to the south. The large Lawrence Hill goods yard was sited to the west of the station. An enlarged goods shed opened in 1895.

In 1984 the line was reduced from four to two tracks and these pass through Lawrence Hill between the western side platform and the former island platform, inter-platform connection for pedestrians being via concrete steps linked to the adjacent road bridge to the south. Limited cover for passengers is today provided by a 'bus shelter' on each of the two platforms. A former access to the old up platform is bricked up on the bridge parapet. Lawrence Hill station was used particularly by residents in other parts of the city travelling to work in the many commercial premises in the area. It was also a departure station for excursions to the south coast and South Wales. Records also indicate that many evacuees from Bristol during the Second World War boarded trains at Lawrence Hill.

Today local passenger services between Bristol Temple Meads and Avonmouth, Severn Beach, Cardiff and Gloucester call at Lawrence Hill. The former goods yard, closed in November 1965, is used by a supermarket (to which there is pedestrian access from the down platform) and as a storage area for building materials. For some years it was used as a car park with part of the site also occupied by a rail connected cement terminal.

In about 1910 passengers throng the up platform waiting for an excursion train to the west country.

THEN Looking north from the Lawrence Hill/Church Road bridge at the extensive facilities comprising two outer platforms and an island platform serving four tracks. The large covered footbridge is a particular feature. The goods shed can be seen to the left of the footbridge.

NOW From a similar position on the road bridge on 22nd March 2005 only two tracks survive with passengers now only served by shelters on the one remaining side platform and western half of the island platform. A supermarket (centre left) covers some of the former goods yard.

THEN A local train travelling south in 1933 alongside the western edge of the island platform and under the impressive footbridge at Lawrence Hill.

NOW Taken from almost exactly the same point the Virgin Voyager ex Newcastle (1027) to Bristol Temple Meads and Penzance passes through the now bleak station on 22nd March 2005.

Montpelier

OPENED: 1st October 1874 (with the opening of the first section of the Clifton Extension Railway to Clifton Down).

CLOSED: Passengers – remains open for services on the Bristol Temple Meads – Avonmouth – Severn Beach line. Goods – 29th November 1965.

Montpelier station opened in October 1874 on the first section of the Clifton Extension Railway to Clifton Down which subsequently opened for passengers through to Avonmouth in 1885. The station is sited on a fairly sharp curve east of the high bridge over Cheltenham Road, 'The Arches'.

The original main buildings on the down (towards Clifton Down) side of the station were in a domestic style of architecture and built of pennant stone with freestone dressings and coigns of yellow stone. Some of the stone was obtained from the railway cutting west of the site at Whiteladies Road. The station master lived above the waiting rooms on the down platform and the GWR and Midland Railway had separate ticket windows. The buildings on the up side principally incorporated waiting rooms.

The original platforms were spacious but largely uncovered, that on the down side being 407 ft long and the up 405 ft; the height of the down platform was 3 ft 1½ inches and the up platform 3 ft 4½ inches. An open iron footbridge linked the platforms and also carried a pedestrian right of way between Cromwell Road and Station Road. In 1883 a coalhouse was provided for the station master at a cost of £40 and four years later, in 1887, an extra bedroom was added for £65. In February 1888 the joint GWR/Midland Railway Committee ruled that the name of the station board should only have one 'L' and not two!

It is recorded that during the 1880s a large number of parcels were handled on the Clifton Extension Railway. Indeed, in 1888 Montpelier handled 3,027 and in 1889 3,184. During the summer of 1888 both Clifton Down and Montpelier stations issued a large number of special tickets to Weston-super-Mare; at Montpelier this totalled 627 adults and 1,038 children, giving an income of £75.6s. Although some way from the Downs, extra traffic was generated in 1886 by the staging of the Bath and West Show. Extra staff at Montpelier included four porters, one clerk and 12 ticket collectors.

By the late nineteenth century it was clear that the station's facilities did not match the level of business; indeed in 1895 a petition had been sent to the joint GWR/MR Committee requesting that the platforms should be better covered, that improved waiting room accommodation should be provided and that a new booking office be built on the up (north side) platform. The companies agreed to extend the canopy on the up platform and improve the waiting room facilities but not to build the additional booking office. The contract was let and work undertaken during 1896. During the First World War the down platform was extended.

In 1903 19 staff were based at Montpelier; the total had fallen to 15 in 1935. At times, before the First World War, extra porters had to be sent to the station. The station was particularly busy with commercial travellers and on Mondays they came with their wares ready for a week's travel by rail. Hampers laden with samples and clothing had to be loaded and extra staff were required to reduce possible delays to train departures. Samples were also sometimes stored at the station over the weekend.

Montpelier goods yard was to the south of the station on the south side of Station Road, accessed by a siding carried on a bridge over the road from the down track. No goods shed was ever provided. Coal traffic brought in for local merchants was the principal activity. Montpelier signal box, with 16 levers, was sited at the west end of the down platform; this controlled access to the yard.

During and after the First World War, Montpelier station closed on Sundays from 1st January 1917 until 15th July 1923. On 29th March 1926 came the first step in the reduction of the station's status when the station master, Mr Denley, was withdrawn, with supervision passing to Clifton Down station. The main station building on the down platform, incorporating the station house, was destroyed in an air raid on 16th March 1941. After the war it was replaced by a low stone building which still stands. In 1950 under the Clifton Down station master, there were still two booking clerks, four porters, a checker and a weighbridge attendant at Montpelier. The goods yard closed on 29th November 1965 and the station became

THEN The main surviving building on the down platform still in railway use in 1957. Signs indicate entrances to the Parcels and Left Luggage Office (centre) and the Ticket Office (right).

NOW Some 48 years later on 1st May 2005 the building remains intact now in use as the premises of 'Period Fireplaces'. A modern metal archway to the left of the building is over the entrance to the one remaining used platform.

unstaffed from 17th July 1967, the signal box had closed earlier that year on 10th May. Today Montpelier remains open on the single track Avonmouth branch with trains calling at the old down (south) platform. All buildings on, and access to, the up platform have now gone; the surviving building on the down platform remains in use for 'Period Fireplaces'. The footbridge and path from Cromwell Road to Station Road continue to give access to the remaining platform. The former goods yard is now a small industrial estate.

THEN A comprehensive view of Montpelier station from the east end in 1928. Note the large tall building on the up platform (right) east of the footbridge and also the platform canopy beyond.

NOW The scene is very different 87 years later on 1st May 2005. A single track on the Avonmouth line runs alongside the former down platform. One old building remains beyond the footbridge, the principal building being destroyed in the Second World War. The disused former up platform remains with no buildings and covered in vegetation. In the distance housing covers former railway land.

Parson Street

OPENED: 29th August 1927 (on the Bristol Temple Meads – Weston-super-Mare – Taunton line originally opened through this site in 1841).

CLOSED: Passengers – remains open for local services on the Bristol Temple Meads – Weston-super-Mare – Taunton line. Goods – facilities never provided.

Parson Street opened in August 1927 as Parson Street 'Platform' on the Bristol to west country line, the principal purpose being to serve local developing suburban areas. Facilities included two small waiting shelters, wooden on the down and metal on the up (towards Temple Meads). Complete rebuilding took place in the early 1930s with the quadrupling of the line from Temple Meads west out of Bristol. Considerable engineering work was undertaken to accommodate four tracks and a station in the space which originally provided for two broad gauge tracks. A short tunnel to the west of the station was eliminated. The two island platforms, with covered waiting shelters, opened on 21st May 1933, the suffix 'Platform'

being dropped. Access to the new station was via two sets of steps from the ticket office on the road bridge to the east of the station.

As well as serving local suburban development for both commuter and excursion traffic, Parson Street station also acted as a minor interchange point for passengers travelling on the Portishead branch. Following the closure for such use of Ashton Gate, Parson Street became, in 1977, the arrival and departure point for special trains conveying 'away' fans to football matches at Ashton Gate, the home of Bristol City Football Club.

The main buildings, including the ticket office, were demolished in January 1971. Today the platforms remain with small basic shelters, brick on the down and metal on the up, with no glass in the windows. The former roof support brackets remain on the steps down to the platforms from the road bridge but the roofs have gone. A limited local passenger service is provided with stopping trains on the Bristol to Weston-super-Mare and Taunton line. In the 2005 timetable six up trains and eight down trains called per weekday during the rush hours, a marginal improvement over previous years.

A close-up of the basic facilities at the original 1927 Platform including the wooden shelter with small fretted canopy on the down platform and a metal shelter on the up (left). Inter platform pedestrian movement is via steps and the road bridge; at the top of the up platform steps there appears to be a small office.

The rebuilt station looking north east towards Bristol Temple Meads in 1963. Wooden shelters serve passengers on the two island platforms; a down DMU approaches under the Parson Street road bridge on which is the booking office.

The booking office on the Parson Street road bridge in March 1965. Notice the prominent letters G.W.

THEN An express runs alongside the down island platform at Parson Street in 1955. The photographer is standing underneath the wooden shelter canopy.

NOW Taken in an almost identical position on the afternoon of 19th March 2005, the Virgin Voyager ex Edinburgh (0810) via Bristol runs through en route to Plymouth. Only two very basic shelters remain to serve passengers using the limited local services. The booking office has gone from the bridge.

Redland

OPENED: 12th April 1897 (on the Bristol Temple Meads – Avonmouth – Severn Beach line, the first section of which opened to Clifton Down through this site in October 1874).

CLOSED: Passengers – remains open for services on the Bristol Temple Meads – Avonmouth – Severn Beach line. Goods – facilities never provided.

Redland station opened in April 1897 on the Clifton Extension Railway which had been opened as far as Clifton Down for passengers in 1874 and through to Avonmouth in 1885. The opening of Redland station was the culmination of much pressure and lobbying. Indeed in October 1885, only one month after the through line to Avonmouth was opened to passengers, a petition was received by the joint GWR and Midland Railway Committee running the line requesting that a station should be provided at a point where the line passed under Lovers Walk in Redland.

A station plan was commissioned but the resulting estimated cost of £3,410 led to action being postponed. Eighteen months later another petition was received and again rejected. In 1892 the Bristol Chamber of Commerce petitioned and the joint Railway Committee (GWR and Midland) replied suggesting that estimated traffic levels did not justify such an expense. However, during the latter part of February 1896, revised plans for a new station were eventually put before the joint Committee and approved. Construction began, providing a facility for a part of Bristol that had been developing very rapidly in the 1880s and 1890s.

The construction of the station was difficult because it needed to take place without disturbing the normal flow of traffic on the line to Avonmouth. The trains carrying materials were unable to remain unloading for a long period and had to cross from the up to the down line or vice versa; on each occasion this meant movements as far as Montpelier station, the nearest crossover point. No special crossover or sidings were laid at the Redland station site.

The west end of the up platform in the 1960s. The nearest bridge carries a public pedestrian way, a continuation of Lovers Walk. The far arch carries a road, Redland Grove. Between these two bridges, the station footbridge links the two platforms and also directly links with the brick booking office (top right).

The station is east of the road bridge carrying Redland Grove over the railway. A pedestrian bridge also crosses the line carrying a continuation of Lovers Walk. Between the two bridges the station footbridge linked the two platforms to the ticket office sited at the north end. Steps led down to the platforms. On the Redland (north side) platform was the station master's office, a general waiting room, a ladies waiting room and cloakrooms, whilst on the down platform (Cotham side) a general waiting shelter only was provided. The total cost of the station, which took about nine months to build, was approximately £2,000.

In spite of bad weather, a fair number of passengers turned up for the departure of the first train from the station at about 7 a.m.; 94 tickets were issued to Clifton Down. In total it was estimated that some 550 passengers booked from Redland on this opening day. A sceptical writer of the time commented that probably few of these were new passengers, but instead had originally been travelling either from Montpelier or Clifton Down stations. In September 1899 a signal box, of a standard Midland Railway design, was opened beyond the east end of the up platform. It closed on 21st June 1950.

In 1903 11 men were employed at Redland. The post of station master did not last many years, being abolished as an economy measure on 27th August 1909, the station being placed under the control of Clifton Down. The total staff had fallen to six by 1938; in 1958, still under Clifton Down, there remained a booking clerk, a porter and a lad porter. From December 1964 Redland became an unstaffed halt after 2 p.m. and became totally unstaffed as from 17th July 1967.

The down track was lifted on 19th October 1970 and thus the Cotham side platform became redundant. The down side shelter, the station footbridge and ticket office were demolished in October 1973 but the down platform was left and remains today, though covered in vegetation. The up platform is still in use on the single track and the main building, including the canopy, remains but not in railway use. Following various uses over the years, in early 2005 it was once again renovated and used by a traditional upholstery firm, Hamilton & Hodson. Access to the platform is from a new entry point through a garage courtyard off South Road.

Staff of the Clifton Extension Railway pose at the station, a ticket collector in the centre. The down side waiting shelter is behind the men.

THEN Looking east in 1964. The principal building at Redland with the station offices is on the up platform (left); a similar design waiting shelter, also with a horizontal canopy, is on the down.

NOW The station in May 2005. The principal building on the former up platform remains though not in railway use. The derelict down platform remains covered in vegetation and bushes, the waiting shelter has long gone.

St Andrews Road

OPENED: 1st March 1917 (on the Avonmouth – Severn Beach – Pilning line originally opened through this site for goods in 1900 and passenger services in 1910).

CLOSED: 13th November 1922.

RE-OPENED: 30th June 1924.

CLOSED: Passengers – remains open as a request stop for passenger services on the Bristol Temple Meads – Avonmouth – Severn Beach line.

St Andrews Road opened in March 1917 as a factory platform on the Filton to Avonmouth line via Henbury. The station, serving the new Avonmouth munitions factory, closed after five years on 13th November 1922 but re-opened in June 1924. The station came into more regular use with the introduction of passenger services on the Severn Beach and Pilning line in 1928. This supplemented the earlier services on the line via Henbury to Filton.

The main facilities were on the up (towards Avonmouth) platform, comprising a long wooden shelter with a wooden canopy and a waiting room. The shelter had been provided for First World War munitions workers. On the down platform two corrugated shelters were added during the Second World War. By the 1980s basic 'bus shelters' on the two platforms served passengers. In the 1990s major rationalisation of track work took place in the area around St Andrews Road station associated with the development of the automated coal depot. Only the original platform on the former down track remains with a small 'bus shelter'; the whole site is dominated by the 200 ft hopper fed by a long conveyor belt from Royal Portbury Dock, a section of which passes under the River Avon. Adjacent to the station footbridge which crosses the tracks to the isolated platform is the office of the EWS Avonmouth Bulk Handling Terminal. Today St Andrews Road is a request stop served by trains (or buses) travelling to and from Severn Beach (seven up and down trains plus eight bus links each way per weekday).

THEN Looking south on 23rd August 1958. Locomotive 2-6-2T No 5532 pulls in with a local train. The original long wooden shelter with a waiting room stands on the up platform (left); the basic shelters on the down platform were added during the Second World War.

THEN Again looking south from the footbridge in May 1989. Two basic 'bus shelters' serve passengers on the double track between Avonmouth and Severn Beach. The overhead pipes are associated with nearby industries.

NOW An even greater transformation has come by 7th April 2005. Major track rationalisation has taken place and now only a single track serves the original down platform on which stands a single shelter. The whole scene, again from the station footbridge, is dominated by the huge loading hopper of the Avonmouth Coal Depot served by a long conveyor from Royal Portbury Dock. A train is passing under the hopper to the left of the picture.

St Annes Park

OPENED: 23rd May 1898 (on the GWR Bristol
Temple Meads – Bath line originally
opened through this site in 1840).

CLOSED: Passengers – 5th January 1970.
Goods – facilities never provided.

St Annes Park opened in May 1898 on the Bristol to Bath Great Western Railway line which had originally been opened to traffic nearly 60 years earlier in 1840. The *Western Daily Press* of Saturday 21st May 1898, an issue incidentally dominated by the death of the Prime Minister, Mr Gladstone, contained a note to the effect that 'The Great Western Railway Company announce that the new station at St Annes Park between Keynsham and Bristol will be opened for traffic on Monday'.

The *Western Daily Press* of 24th May 1898 contained the following report of the opening: 'The new suburban station about 1¼ miles from Bristol on the Great Western Railway which is known as St Annes Park, opened yesterday, the first train to stop being the 6.35 from Temple Meads. The station is situated amidst delightful surroundings within a stone's throw of the charming St Annes Wood and only a few minutes walk from Conham which is a favourite boating resort for Bristolians during the summer months. It will not only serve to take people into the country with a journey of only a few minutes duration, but it will also be the means of opening up an important residential area. The credit of developing the estate and securing the railway service belongs to Mr James Sinnott who has not only exerted his influence with the railway company but has been to considerable expense in the matter.' The paper went on to report that one of the passengers on the early train was the same Mr Sinnott and, as this first train steamed into the station, a salute of 25 fog signals was fired. The paper

A view looking looking east at the station opened in 1898 serving the nearby developing housing areas. The gentleman is standing on the down platform awaiting a local train to Temple Meads. Note the attractive small flower beds surrounded by whitened stones.

Looking west towards Bristol Temple Meads in July 1963. The buildings, very impressive for a suburban station, are connected by a covered footbridge. Passengers enter and leave the station at the footbridge level; the canopy over the entrance is seen top right.

described the station in the following terms: 'The building which has been constructed of local stone is of substantial character and consists of a booking office and parcels office on the level of the bridge and up and down platforms each having a Ladies and General Waiting Room completely furnished.' It noted that 12 trains in each direction stop at the station except on Sundays when the number would be reduced to seven. The cost of the facilities was estimated to be some £4,000.

This early report gives a good indication of the significant facilities provided and St Annes Park station was of a surprisingly large scale considering its close proximity to Temple Meads. Every comfort was offered to passengers from the nearby residential area. The impressive buildings on each platform were connected by a covered footbridge. A signal box, at the west end of the up platform, opened nine years before the station in 1889; it closed on 4th February 1909 when it amalgamated with the Bristol Temple Meads East Depot box.

In its early days the station played the dual role of serving the local residential population and providing access to local beauty spots. The latter

role began to fade with the introduction of the motor car and for much of its later life St Annes Park served merely as a commuter station for passengers travelling to either Bristol or Bath. The number of passenger tickets issued rose from 21,506 in 1903 to a maximum of 72,803 in 1930 but then fell to 50,305 in 1933. In 1898, the year the station opened, there were eight staff (station master, one ticket collector, two porters, one lad porter and three signal men). There were nine staff in 1903 but the total fell to five over the period 1913 to 1933. Surprisingly, in view of the size of the station, no freight facilities were provided, though parcels were handled. St Annes Park station was unstaffed from 6th March 1967 and closed on 5th January 1970, somewhat later than many of the other suburban station closures in Bristol, when local services between Bristol and Bath were withdrawn. No lineside trace remains; the former Station Road off St Annes Park Road is now sealed off by a locked steel gate. Through the gate setts of the old approach road and a pavement edge can still be seen as can a section of railway fence to the north-east side of the old road.

THEN Looking down and east from Wick Road bridge at St Annes Park in July 1963. A GWR Hall locomotive hauls a down train through the station having emerged from Bristol No 2 tunnel. The sidings (left) link back to the Bristol East depot through the deep cutting which resulted from the opening up of Bristol No 1 tunnel in 1887.

NOW 42 years later the view from the Wick Road bridge on 21st March 2005. The ex London Paddington (1300) to Bristol Temple Meads service passes through the former site of the station; no line-side trace remains.

St Philips

OPENED: 2nd May 1870 (as the terminus of a
            new spur from the Midland Railway's
            Bristol – Gloucester line).
CLOSED: Passengers – 21st September 1953.
            Goods – 1st April 1967.

St Philips station opened in May 1870 as a terminus for the Midland Railway's local services, in particular those running on the line to and from Bath Green Park. The station was provided to relieve growing congestion at Bristol Temple Meads.

The station was sited on the extreme northern edge of the Midland Railway's large goods yard; this yard, completed in 1866 and covering some six acres, included a substantial goods shed (180 ft x 133 ft). The main wooden station building with a typical Midland Railway ridge and furrowed glass roof stood on the single face platform and appeared to have been constructed at minimum cost, probably because of the financial problems of the Midland Railway in the early 1870s. There was, however, a large booking office with some waiting space in the booking hall. The waiting room itself was often used by the goods department to store documents. The entrance to the booking hall was at the foot of the sloping approach in granite setts down from the appropriately named Midland Road.

Trains at St Philips were almost entirely local serving Fishponds, Mangotsfield, Warmley and Bath. The principal advantage of St Philips station, sited adjacent to Midland Road and Waterloo Road, was its proximity to the Old Market shopping area though this advantage obviously declined after many of the buildings and shops in that street were destroyed in the Second World War. The local trains brought not only shoppers but also commuters into the centre of Bristol and even in the early 1950s were well used for the latter purpose. Some 13 local trains a day came, via Mangotsfield, into

Looking east from the terminal buffers in 1948. A local train, probably bound for Bath, stands at the wooden platform over which the canopy looks in need of repair. To the right is the northern edge of the large goods yard.

THEN Looking west along the slightly curved platform in the early 1950s shortly before St Philips station closed to passengers. Staff pose beside the milepost which reads 130¾, the distance to Derby London Road junction (all Midland Railway distances were recorded from Derby. MR 'up' platforms also indicated those used for travel towards that town). Waterloo Garage stands high above the station in Waterloo Road.

NOW The same view on 20th April 2005. The high stone wall behind the station seen in the previous photograph remains; the station site is occupied by Walsall Electrical Distributors on the Kingsland Trading Estate which occupies much of the original goods yard.

A rather dark, but the only known, picture of the station entrance in about 1923. The granite setts approach leads down from the junction of the appropriately named Midland Road and Waterloo Road.

St Philips with most trains being concentrated in the morning and evening rush hours. In the 1950s these local trains were diverted to Temple Meads and St Philips closed to passenger traffic on 21st September 1953. Prior to this there was closure on Sundays. A gas leak apparently caused an explosion resulting in damage to the buildings before their actual closure. Traffic continued at the adjacent goods yard for another 14 years until 1st April 1967.

Today there is no trace of the station, the site of which is now occupied by the premises of Walsall Electrical Distributors on the Kingsland Trading Estate, which now covers the former goods yard. The high stone wall which overlooked the station to the north still stands on the south side of Waterloo Road. The name Midland Road provides us with the sole reminder of the early railway history.

Sea Mills

OPENED: 6th March 1865 (with the opening of the Bristol Port Railway and Pier line Hotwells – Avonmouth).

CLOSED: Passengers – remains open for services on the Bristol Temple Meads – Avonmouth – Severn Beach line. Goods – services not provided of any scale (see text).

Sea Mills opened in March 1865 as a simple south-west facing structure on the original single track Hotwells to Avonmouth line. A small timber building containing a booking office and porter's office faced on to an uncovered platform. This original platform was doubled in length to 300 ft in 1878 as part of a deal agreed with the Board of Trade that a station need not be provided at Sneyd Park Junction following opening of the Clifton Extension Railway.

Sea Mills was rebuilt in association with track doubling on the section of the line between Shirehampton and Sneyd Park Junction, completed and opened on 6th January 1907. As a part of this rebuilding a second platform was added, both platforms now being about 330 ft long. The buildings were rebuilt in a rather unusual domestic style, the impressive up platform building (with a date on the rear wall of 1906) featured an arched terracotta entrance and spar covered walls. The roof was high pitched and overlain with Broseley tiles. It incorporated a booking hall, booking office, ladies waiting room and w.c. Also on the up platform was a gent's urinal and w.c. On the down platform a small general waiting room was erected. Rebuilding also

THEN An excellent clear record of the buildings looking north west in 1964. The double track continues over the River Trym bridge towards Shirehampton. On the up platform (right) are the impressive 1906 station building and the 1894 station house. A waiting shelter with a small chimney stands on the down platform.

included the construction of a subway at the west end under the line linked with a path to the towpath along the river bank. One of the tasks undertaken by the porter at Sea Mills was to clean rubbish out of the public subway after high tides. 'Dirty money' was paid for this operation and the railway company provided a hosepipe and wellington boots for the job! There was no footbridge at Sea Mills though the station had a barrow crossing and a public level crossing.

In 1894 a station master's house was built very close to the up buildings at a cost of £240. It is recorded that at around the turn of the century the station master at Sea Mills kept poultry, a cow and pigs and used his pony and trap to fetch swill from the docks. He sold eggs to passengers and provided the superintendent at Bristol with butter and eggs. At a later date these practices ceased as the station came under the Shirehampton station master who was provided with tide tables so that he could check on the 'dirty money' claims from the Sea Mills porter! In 1923 staffing levels were at

their highest at six; this figure continued until about 1935. In the 1950s, then under the Shirehampton station master, there were two porters and two lad porters; by 1961 there were only two porters and this had reduced to one by 1965.

In the early days Sea Mills station had a goods siding but no goods yard or shed. For most of its life it only handled passenger traffic. In later years a lorry came from Temple Meads to collect and deliver parcels at Sea Mills and Shirehampton stations. The original pattern of one track alongside the up platform was re-established with the singling of the line from Ashley Hill to Avonmouth on 19th October 1970. The down platform is abandoned but still in situ covered in vegetation; the building has gone. The principal building on the up platform is still in existence being used by an engineering firm, whilst immediately adjacent stands Station House, in residential use. The platform itself is provided with two small shelters (one brick and one metal and glass) serving passengers on the Avonmouth and Severn Beach line.

NOW Looking north west at the remaining former up platform on 3rd April 2005. The brick and glass/metal shelters serve passengers whilst behind are the surviving former station house and station building.

THEN Looking south east from the rail bridge over the River Trym close to its confluence with the River Avon. It is probably the station master standing in front of his house with the impressive 1906 station building to his right.

NOW Taken on 6th June 2005, also from the River Trym bridge, the now single track passes the original up platform. The station building and station house have changed little but are no longer in railway use. Two small shelters serve the passengers. The remains of the former down platform lie derelict covered with vegetation (right).

Shirehampton

OPENED: 6th March 1865 (with the opening of the Bristol Port Railway and Pier line Hotwells – Avonmouth).

CLOSED: Passengers – remains open for services on the Bristol Temple Meads – Avonmouth/Severn Beach line. Goods – 29th November 1965.

Shirehampton was the venue for the turning of the first sod of the Bristol Port Railway and Pier line on 19th February 1863. The ceremony in a marquee erected in a field owned by the Chairman of the Company was performed by the then Mayoress of Bristol, Mrs S. V. Hare. About 120 guests sat down for an excellent meal in the National School Room.

Shirehampton, like Sea Mills, opened in March 1865 as a south facing facility on the single track Hotwells to Avonmouth line. At a crossing loop there was one platform on the northern side of the line. Shirehampton station was the first headquarters of the Bristol Port Railway and the construction and style of architecture was, as a result, superior to that of other stations of the line. The original building contained a booking office, the superintendent of the line's office and the porter's room. The platform was covered along the length of the building. In 1893 this northern platform was lengthened by the GWR to 235 ft at a cost of £285 and at about the same time the station master's house was built a little to the west of the station buildings on the up side. From 1875 a single road locomotive depot, replacing the

A view east soon after the redevelopment of the station in 1903. Passengers stand on the north side up platform. The two sections of the up side building can be distinguished by the different size and style of the platform canopy. A fine open lattice type footbridge connects the two platforms.

shed that had burnt down at Hotwells, was sited at the east end of the station. In 1900 it also burnt down and from January 1905 was replaced by a depot at Avonmouth.

At the time of track doubling from Avonmouth Dock to Shirehampton in 1903 (into use 16th May) remodelling of the station took place; the main station building on the up platform was extended to include comfortable waiting rooms and the canopy was also extended. A new down platform was constructed with a kiosk-like waiting room and, to connect the two platforms, a wide open footbridge was erected. Also included in this development was a small goods yard and coal sidings on the up north side behind the station. In 1921 an extra siding was added for conveyance of material from the adjacent premises of R. Brodie for construction work on the Portway. A signal box at the east end of the down platform with 20 levers was in use until October 1970 when the line was singled.

The commencement of passenger services in 1865 had unusual circumstances in that the incumbent of Shirehampton church and some parishioners pleaded that trains should not run on a Sunday. As a result, although trains ran on the line, they did not stop at Shirehampton station. However, within a month, a petition had been made against this practice and by May 1865 new timetables had been issued which included stops on Sundays at Shirehampton.

During the First World War 14,000 wagons associated with the nearby Re-Mount horse depot, were received at Shirehampton; up to 60 a day were dealt with – mostly filled with hay or saw-dust for the horses. About 12 wagons a day were despatched carrying manure, some going to Cadbury Road station on the Weston, Clevedon and Portishead Light Railway. On 7th September 1915 the King and Queen passed through Shirehampton station en route to a local troop depot.

Before 1920 Shirehampton had a station master, three clerks and four porters; in the 1930s staff levels averaged 10; by 1958 there was a station master, two clerks, two leading porters and a porter. Shirehampton station closed to goods traffic in November 1965 and became unstaffed from 17th July 1967. A storage tank for domestic fuel oil was built in the station's goods yard with deliveries made by rail over the period 1980-1985. Buildings on the old up platform remained in a surprisingly good condition in use as offices, with a canopy in place, for some years but, following a fire in the 1990s, they were demolished and replaced with a brick shelter with a wooden fretted edge canopy. The down platform was abandoned following the singling of the line from Ashley Hill to Avonmouth on 19th October 1970. The station remains open for trains running on the Avonmouth and Severn Beach line. The old down platform is still there, covered in undergrowth, but the shelter has gone. The former goods yard has been completely redeveloped, the principal occupant in 2005 being MHS Highway Hire Company. A small station car park with 10 spaces has been laid out. The former station master's house remains in residential use; its garden incorporates a small brick building with a decorative chimney surviving from the former station buildings.

Staff pose for the camera in about 1921. Unusually three of them are wearing trilby hats instead of railway caps.

THEN A much later view east in 1964 taken from the up platform of Shirehampton under the footbridge. The two sections of the up side canopy can again be seen (left). On the down side platform stands the kiosk-like waiting room and signal box.

NOW Taken almost at the same spot on 4th April 2005, a shelter with a wooden canopy serves passengers on the remaining former up platform with the derelict remains of the former down platform to the right. Houses in Dursley Road provide some continuity between the then and now photos.

THEN Looking west from the east end of the up platform; the signal box and shelter are on the down platform with the lattice footbridge at the far end.

NOW A view west from about the identical position on the remaining former up platform. The 1452 train to Avonmouth on 4th April 2005 stands beside the shelter. The remains of the redundant former down platform are clearly visible to the left.

Stapleton Road

OPENED: 8th September 1863 (with the opening of the Bristol and South Wales Union Railway Bristol Temple Meads – New Passage Pier).

CLOSED: Passengers – remains open for local services on the Bristol – Gloucester, Cardiff and Avonmouth/Severn Beach lines.
Goods – 29th November 1965.

Stapleton Road station originally opened in September 1863 with one platform on the west side of the single track Bristol and South Wales Union Railway line. Doubling of the section of line from Temple Meads through Stapleton Road took place in 1874 to facilitate the running of trains on the new Clifton Extension Railway. A second platform was added east of the two tracks. In early 1888 the section north from Stapleton Road to Narroways Hill Junction was quadrupled to accommodate extra traffic, separate tracks being allocated for the South Wales and Avonmouth trains. In November 1891 further quadrupling of the tracks south of Stapleton Road was completed. The buildings, as normally remembered, date from rebuilding associated with these track changes in the late 1880s and early 1890s. They stood on two long outer platforms and a long central island platform served by the four tracks.

The main station building including the booking office was on the St Marks Church, Easton (up) side, linked by a large covered footbridge to the other platforms on all of which were substantial buildings with canopies of varying scale and design. A refreshment room was sited on the middle island platform. A goods yard was sited on the down side north of the railway bridges over Stapleton Road.

Stapleton Road became one of Bristol's busiest stations. In particular it was the main stopping point in Bristol for the south coast to South Wales steam hauled trains that did not call at Temple Meads but travelled direct via Dr Day's Junction. It was also an exchange point for passengers on the Clifton Extension Railway from Clifton and Avonmouth wishing to join trains to South Wales and the south coast. Special connections were also made at Stapleton Road with through excursion trains on the South Wales line and many excursionists started their trips from here. During the Second World War

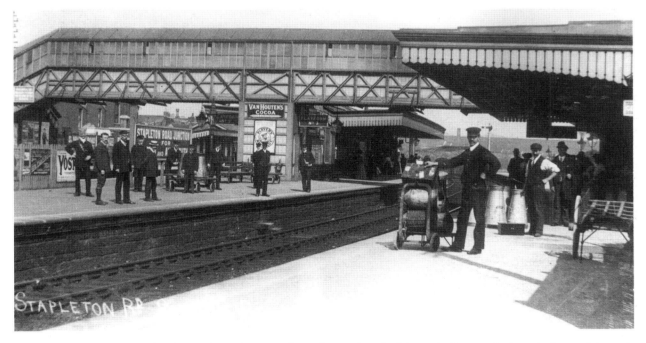

An atmospheric photograph taken early in the 1900s from the south end of the main line up platform in front of the main offices. Note all the staff, the variety of trolleys, milk churns and metal advertisements.

THEN Standard Class 2-6-2T No 82044 arrives with the 4.37 pm to Bristol from Severn Beach on 24th August 1958. Stopping under the surviving footbridge it is alongside the west side of the island platform used for local services. The large shelters with canopies on the island platform have gone by this time.

NOW Taken from about the same point some 47 years later on 28th March 2005 the eight car Virgin Voyager from Glasgow (1005) to Bristol and Penzance passes the skeleton remains of the footbridge which now only links the former down local side platform and the west side of the island platform. All other structures have gone.

The principal station building on the east side of the station at the head of the approach road from Stapleton Road. A Jaguar car stands in front on 13th March 1964. The extreme east end of the fine covered footbridge can be seen to the right of the building and left of the lamp post.

The arrival of Prime Minister Lloyd George recorded outside the main building in this historic photograph of about 1920.

An excellent clear view north along the central island platform taken in 1963. The large covered footbridge spans the two local line tracks (left) and the two main line tracks (right). The main station building with tall chimneys is on the right.

a number of evacuees from Bristol departed from Stapleton Road. Gradually however, the role of the station declined, in particular with the re-routeing of all south coast to South Wales trains into Temple Meads made easier by the introduction of diesel multiple units that can readily reverse direction. A continuing use of Stapleton Road was for supporters travelling to Bristol Rovers F.C. matches when the team was based at Eastville Stadium.

Today Stapleton Road station is a sad sight with all the major buildings gone, the only remains being a section of the now uncovered footbridge linking the platforms, only two of which are in use serving local trains on the Avonmouth, Cardiff and Gloucester lines. Recent modern metal and glass shelters provide cover and metal benches are provided on each platform. A notable feature is a colourful mural on the back wall of the down platform painted in August 1999 illustrating features of local life in east Bristol. Rubble fills some of the former trackbed between the old up platform and east face of the island, the access path to the truncated footbridge crossing the rubble between two metal fences. Remnants of road setts and pavement edges can be seen adjacent to the site of the former main building on the east side. The M32 motorway now passes through the southern end of the former goods yard. Goods facilities at Stapleton Road were withdrawn in November 1965. The number of tracks through Stapleton Road was reduced to two as from 20th February 1984, resuming the position of some 100 years earlier.

Further Reading

Binding J., *Brunel's Bristol Temple Meads*, Oxford
  Publishing Company 2001
Burgess N., *The Best Way to Bath*, R.P. Printing,
  1984
Dowling G. and Whitehouse J., *British Railways Past and
  Present No 16, Avon, Cotswolds and the Malverns*,
  Silver Link Publishing, 1993
Hale M., *'Twixt London and Bristol*, Oxford Publishing
  Company, 1985
Harris M. (Ed), *Brunel, the GWR and Bristol*, Ian Allan,
  1985
Harris P., *Bristol's 'Railway Mania 1862–1864'*, Bristol
  Branch of the Historical Association, 1987
Maggs C.G., *Branch Lines of Gloucestershire*, Alan
  Sutton, 1991
  Branch Lines of Somerset, Alan Sutton, 1993
  Bristol Railway Panorama, Millstream Books, 1990
  Rail Centres: Bristol, Ian Allan, 1st Edition 1981,
    2nd Edition 1996
  The Bristol and Gloucester Railway, Oakwood Press,
    1st Edition 1969, 2nd enlarged Edition 1992
  The Bristol Port Railway and Pier, Oakwood Press,
    1975
  The GWR Bristol to Bath Line, Sutton Publishing,
    2001
Meason G., *The Illustrated Guide to the Great Western
  Railway 1852*, Reprinted 1983

Mitchell V., and Smith K., Middleton Press (various
  publication dates)
  Bath Green Park to Bristol, 1999
  Branch Lines around Avonmouth, 2004
  Branch Lines to Clevedon and Portishead, 2003
  Bristol to Taunton, 2003
  Frome to Bristol, 1986
  Gloucester to Bristol, 2004
  Swindon to Bristol, 2002
Norris J., *The Bristol and South Wales Union Railway*,
  Railway and Canal Historical Society, 1985
Smith M., *The Railways of Bristol and Somerset*, Ian
  Allan, 1992
Thomas E., *Down the Mouth, A History of Avonmouth*,
  Ethel Thomas, 2nd Edition, 1992
Vaughan A., *Great Western Architecture, A Pictorial
  Record*, Oxford Publishing Company, 1977
Vincent M., *Lines to Avonmouth*, Oxford Publishing
  Company, 1979
  Reflections on the Portishead Branch, Oxford
    Publishing Company, 1983
  Through Countryside and Coalfield, Oxford
    Publishing Company, 1990
Wray A., *Memories of the Mangotsfield to Bath Branch*,
  Avon Valley Railway, 1988

Acknowledgements

The author is very grateful for the permission received to use photographs from the following collections:

Lens of Sutton (inc photographs taken by J.L. Smith, the owner of Lens of Sutton) pages: 42, 65 (right), 89, 106 (top)
Stations UK pages: 35, 52 (top), 53, 56, 57, 58 (top), 59 (top), 66, 70, 71 (top), 82 (top), 87 (top), 88 (top), 91 (top), 99, 100, 105 (top), 110
National Railway Museum/LGRP pages: 33 (top), 54 (top), 68 (top), 74 (top), 81 (top), 97, 98
Colin Maggs pages: 14, 18, 22 (bottom), 27 (top), 69, 73 (bottom), 104
Mike Tozer pages: 15, 17, 19 (top & bottom), 20 (bottom), 22 (top), 23, 24, 32 (top & bottom), 34, 48 (top), 51 (top & middle), 62 (top), 67, 75, 76 (bottom), 77 (top), 78 (left), 90, 94, 102 (top), 107, 109 (bottom)

Brunel University Mowat Collection pages: 72, 85 (top)
P.J. Garland (via Roger Carpenter) pages: 64 (top), 87 (bottom), 95, 96 (top)
Roger Carpenter page: 26 (top)
R.K. Blencowe page: 65 (left)
Michael Hale pages: 44, 73 (top), 92, 108 (top)
P.J. Kelley page: 29 (top)
G.A. Nicholls page: 38
J. D. Fisher page: 31
Peter Davey page: 20 (top)

The remaining photographs were taken by the author or are from his own collection where the copyright owner is unknown or unclear. Prints from the Brunel University Transport Collection are available from W.R. Burton, 3 Fairway, Clifton, York YO30 5QA.